ERRATA

page 1
line 3

Copying — An Old Practice

page 57
line 7

(Copr. or © in addition to the name of the copy-

page 114
lines 10-18

a. Profit Maximization.   The first pricing policy is based on maximizing profit (π), which results from the difference between total revenue (R) and total cost (C):

$$\pi = R - C$$

Assuming that the demand function is linear, the demand curve can be stated as follows:

$$P = a + bQ$$

where $a > 0$ (positive), $b < 0$ (negative), P is price, and Q is quantity

page 115
line 4

where $F > 0$ (positive), $V < 0$ (negative), F is prerun

page 116
lines 1& 2

where F and V and $a > 0$ (positive) and $b < 0$ (negative).

figure at bottom of page

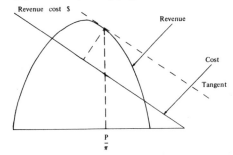

page 117
line 4

curve.   Therefore, $\frac{P}{\pi}$ is the price a commercial publisher

line 17

and since the maximum profit is at the point $\frac{P}{\pi}$ where

(equation at bottom of page)

$$\frac{P}{\pi} = \frac{a + V}{2}$$

page 118
figure

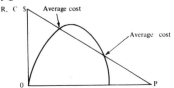

CRISIS IN COPYRIGHT

BOOKS IN

LIBRARY AND INFORMATION SCIENCE

A Series of Monographs and Textbooks

EDITOR

ALLEN KENT

Director, Office of Communications Programs
University of Pittsburgh
Pittsburgh, Pennsylvania

Additional volumes in preparation

CRISIS IN COPYRIGHT

William Z. Nasri

University of Pittsburgh
Pittsburgh, Pennsylvania

MARCEL DEKKER, INC.　　　　New York and Basel

MARCEL DEKKER, INC.
270 Madison Avenue, New York, New York 10016

LIBRARY OF CONGRESS CATALOG CARD NUMBER: 0-8247-75-43046
ISBN: 0-8247-6401-3

Current Printing (last digit):
10 9 8 7 6 5 4 3 2 1

PRINTED IN THE UNITED STATES OF AMERICA

To My Wife Eunice
And Our Children
Nadine And William

FOREWORD

Man's struggle to maintain freedom of action has traditionally been confounded by the need of society to impose controls. This need finds its rationale in attempting to assure that individual freedom does not impinge too much on the rights of others.

The freedom to read is now accepted as the right of any individual, and attempts to limit this right often lead to legal tests. But how far this right extends is a question that has become increasingly important and interesting as technology has made it possible and even cost effective to copy published materials, to record the materials in computer-processible form, and to transmit images of the published materials over considerable distances.

When an individual purchases a book, it is said that he owns the book. But what are the rights of ownership? To destroy the book—certainly! To loan the book—probably, at least precedent in libraries suggest this right. But to copy or transmit parts or all of the material is the sticking point insofar as ownership rights are concerned—because here impingement on the rights of the publisher may eventually be at risk.

The issue has many facets; the need to resolve it is timely. What is really required is the introduction of objective data so that light can be shed on the issue, to partially substitute for the heat of emotions. For example, it is necessary to know whether photocopying does indeed affect the economics of publishing. If it does, then to what extent. Once this is known the basis can be established for considering whether fees must be collected.

If fees are to be collected, how will the library be affected? Will the public interest be served, or will it have a deleterious effect?

Who is obliged to collect a fee—the library or the publisher? Who is entitled to participate in the funds accrued—the publisher, the author, the library?

The question also must be asked about the fate of the publishing or information industry if fees are established, or not. Similarly, what will be the fate of the library if distribution rights, by photocopying or otherwise, are compromised.

This book takes a step toward shedding light on the issue, through the analysis of publishing economics, copyright legislation, legal tests, and objective data acquired on journal photocopying.

Allen Kent

INTRODUCTION

When the present copyright law was enacted in 1909, the problem of photo-copying copyrighted works did not exist. The issue came into being with the introduction of copying machines which are capable not only of transferring and replicating copyrighted materials quickly and in quantity, but also of making copies which, in themselves, are adaptable for the production of further copies. The problem has intensified in recent years with the progressive development of relatively inexpensive copying machines which have simplified and greatly extended the practice of photocopying among scholars, researchers, students, and librarians. The implications of this phenomenon on the copyright law have a direct bearing upon the dissemination of information in general and scientific and technical information in particular. With the "explosion of information" and the flood of materials since the Sputnik era, library photocopying is becoming essential in the effective dissemination and use of information for research or casual study. The urgent and serious needs of readers and libraries in this area are manifested in the library clientele's demands; the vast number of research projects; the government and foundation grants in support of such projects; and the government's policies and aid to libraries in support of photocopying.

The publishing industry may have a moral obligation to disseminate knowledge but it also has a "business or legal obligation" to stockholders, employees, dealers, and clients to stay afloat by realizing profits that will in turn enable publishers to fulfill their moral obligation toward the public. Copyright law is an incentive to the authors and their assigns (usually publishers) to create and disseminate knowledge. It is, in essence, a monopoly, a tradeoff, or a price that society has to pay in return for the advancement of science and useful arts. Statutory copyright, therefore, is based on a profit motive for both the author and the entrepreneur. The question is whether the interest of the copyright owner is sufficient to warrant the extension of the copyright monopoly to cover library photocopying.

Copyright owners in the United States, for some years, have been complaining about an accelerating decline in sales and no increase, if not loss, of subscriptions. Consequently, smaller sales and fewer subscriptions have resulted in higher prices, which contribute further to smaller sales and fewer subscriptions. Other contributing factors are the following:

1. The continuous cuts in library and operating budgets due to inflation

2. The rise in wages of librarians and in operational costs of libraries and their effect on the budget for acquisition

3. The new technology and particularly photocopying as practiced by libraries and researchers

Curtis Benjamin of McGraw-Hill Company admitted that "no one can prove conclusively just how much these new practices have hurt the sales. . . . However, publishers can clearly discern progressive changes for the worse in the pattern of library purchase. . . . They can also discern that the progression has worsened sharply in recent years, when the copying practices became more prevalent."*

The publishers' answer to the problem has been a continuous acceleration of prices and the use of smaller formats. This was the result of the dual impact of inflated dollar costs and depressed sales, with the latter encouraging photocopying. However, in the last two decades, vast increases in research funding resulted in a great increase in materials published to report the findings of research projects. A further result was that no one individual can subscribe to more than a fraction of the journals published in almost any given field. In addition, there is only so much time that a scientist or researcher can spend on reading.

In order to determine if photocopying has an adverse effect on the actual or potential market for copyrighted work, one has to determine if photocopying serves as a substitute for a subscription to any given journal. The court case of *The Williams & Wilkins Company* v. *the United States* exemplifies the controversy over publishers' claims that the decline in sale of subscriptions is due to library photocopying. The four journals in suit are, as per the plaintiff's choice and claim, an exemplification of the said actual

---

* Curtis G. Benjamin, "Soaring Prices and Sinking Sales of Scientific Monographs." *Science* 183:283 (Jan. 25, 1974).

and potential losses. The chairman of the board of the Williams & Wilkins Company and the National Institutes of Health and the National Library of Medicine experts agreed on the difficulty of proof because of the lack of studies concerning this claim.†

The question to be reviewed in this book is whether commercial publishers of scientific and technical periodicals lose subscriptions because of reprography. Thus, it is necessary to examine the development of photocopying and its influence on library operations and services and to discuss the economics of publishing.

---

† *The Williams & Wilkins Company* v. *the United States*, The United States Government of Claims, Report of Commissioner James F. Davis to the Court, No. 73-68, Feb. 16, 1972.

CONTENTS

CRISIS IN COPYRIGHT

Chapter 1

BACKGROUND OF THE PROBLEM

Copying – An Old Problem

Copying is an old practice and was included in St. Benedict's Rule as a virtuous activity. Gutenberg's invention of printing was regarded primarily "as an advance in the art of copying ... and was duly opposed by the scribes...."(1) Nevertheless, printing continued to develop and to spread all over the world.

By the mid-16th century, the leading printers in London formed the Stationer's Company.(2) In 1556 a royal decree emanating from the Catholic Queen Mary secured monopoly to the Stationer's Company over all printing as a means of controlling the spread of Protestantism and the Reformation.

> Printing was subject to the order of the Star Chamber, and all published works had to be entered in the register of the Stationer's Company and in the name of some particular member of that Company, who forever after had the sole right to publish that work.(3)

The statutory copyright, therefore, was a product of censorship and trade regulation and not a product of common law, as the court did not see it as a concept to deal with complex issues. It was intended, in essence, to control the press and not to protect the rights of the authors.

1

The first law to recognize the author's right was the Statute of Anne, which was enacted in 1710. It was an "Act for the Encouragement of Learning by Vesting the Copies of Printed Books in the Authors or Purchasers of such Copies During the Times Therein Mentioned."(4)   The Statute of Anne was, and still is, the prototype of all subsequent copyright legislation in almost every nation, including the United States.

In the U.S. Constitution, the Congress was given the power "to promote the progress of science and useful arts, by securing for limited times to authors and inventors the exclusive right to their respective writings and discoveries."(5)   Pursuant to this power, Congress passed the first copyright act on 13 May 1790, modeled after the Statute of Anne "for the encouragement of learning, by securing the copies of maps, charts and books, to the authors and proprietors of such copies."   The period of protection was for 14 years plus an additional renewal term of 14 years.   In 1802, Congress extended the copyright protection to "arts of designing, engraving ... and other prints."   In 1821 the copyright law was revised to include the right to musical compositions and to extend the duration of copyright to 28 years, renewable for an additional 14 years.   The law passed through several amendments, the last of which became effective on 1 July 1909, in which the period of renewal was changed to 28 years.   This amendment also established the Office of the Register of Copyrights under the Librarian of Congress.   In 1947 the Copyright Act of 1909 was amended and became law as Title 17 of the U.S. Code.(6)   The new act, which is our current copyright law, did not make substantive changes in the 1909 law other than "rearranging its subject matter and omitting obsolete provisions."(7)   One can assume, therefore, that the copyright law has not been basically revised since 1909. Many jurists regard the present law, for example, as "Byzantine," filled with "silly and anachronistic provisions" and "senseless rigidities and ambiguities."(8)

The thrust of the 1909 copyright law, however, was greatly affected by dramatic technological developments. New inventions, techniques, and methods of communication, storing, reproducing, and disseminating the various types of works that are the subject matter of copyright emerged, and it became obvious that the copyright law, as it stands, is unable to accommodate the extraordinary technological, industrial, and commercial changes that have taken place since 1909 and will certainly continue to develop in the future.

For instance, the operation of photocopying machines is being made easier, faster, and less expensive per copy. Any amount of published work can be easily duplicated by the push of a button to the point that in 1966 Professor Marshall McLuhan, addressing the Congress of Poets, Playwrights, Editors, Essayists and Novelists (PEN), proclaimed that "in the age of Xerox, the reader becomes a publisher and so does the schoolroom."(9) Computers and data banks are means for storing and retrieving the vast amount of information in all fields for research purposes. Confronted with the explosion of information in different forms, the user welcomes every possible technological innovation to cope with the flood of information which he cannot afford not to know.

Libraries and information centers also serve as repositories and distributors of information. Their product is service and their functions can be summarized in three points:

1. To acquire information in diverse forms (for example, books, journals, photorecords, and films)

2. To process this information and make it readily available to the user

3. To disseminate information on demand to the user (for example, in house use, lending, and reproduction)

A library can be defined as a place that "houses a collection of books, manuscripts, and other materials to preserve them and make them available for use."(10) Libraries are established to provide numerous services to users.   Service, therefore, is the most important function of libraries, which have become indispensable in today's world, for "as society became increasingly information-based, and as the storing of complex bodies of information became more essential to every aspect of its management, and indeed to the individual functioning within the society, the library became a more essential operating component of the society."(11)   As knowledge becomes more extensive, it is increasingly necessary that it be collected in a manner that makes it available to the general public and to those with a special purpose.

Library materials are powerful in themselves, and that power varies with the quality of information contained in each item in the library.   Its full potency, however, can be seen and achieved only when the item is made readily available to the user.   Consequently, one of the main roles of the library is to make accessible all available information within the limits of the library's financial and physical resources.   Conversely, a library falls short of its function when it is unable to provide its users with the information that is available in any given field, assuming that the library's resources enable it to acquire this type of information. The user's satisfaction hinges on many factors, the most important of which is the library budget. The goal of increasing the number of titles and copies to the "satisfaction point" cannot be achieved without realistic economic practice.(12) The cost of purchasing books and subscriptions to journals is usually accompanied by increased staff cost. Balancing the library budget while meeting the pressing demands of patrons depends on many factors, one of which is the duplication and reproduction of library material.

Next to the lending of materials, the most frequently used library service may now be photoduplication. The introduction of xerographic equipment after World War II, in addition to the information explosion of the post-Sputnik era, made copying a mass service, and a study has suggested that "libraries are changing from lending institutions to reprinting institutions."(13)

The unabridged *Webster's Third International Dictionary* defines a photocopy as "a negative or positive photographic reproduction of graphic matter (as drawing or printing)." The *Oxford English Dictionary* defines "copying" as "the action of the verb copy." It also defines "copy" as "an imitation of anything; a reproduction of an original and, in a sense, copy reflects plenty and abundance (copious quantity."(14) *Black's Law Dictionary* defines "copy" as a "transcript or a double of an original writing."(15)

Copying can be done by hand or by a machine. The first mechanical duplicator of documents was invented late in the 19th century by Thomas Alva Edison. Mr. Dick of A. B. Dick Company of Chicago, a former lumberman who became bored with copying his price list by hand, obtained the rights to produce and market Edison's mimeograph.(16) The machine did not sell well because people did not want more than one or two copies of office documents or, as was stated to Mr. Dick, "Why should I want to have a lot of copies of this and that lying around? Nothing but clutter in the office, a temptation to prying eyes and a waste of good paper."(17) The first users of the machine were nonbusiness organizations (for example, churches, schools, and Boy Scout groups). By 1890 the typewriter and carbon paper had become common. Mimeographing became a standard office procedure at the turn of the century, and by 1940 half a million mimeotraph devices were in use.(18) The offset printing press, which was invented in 1930, competed successfully because it provided a better copy with greater ease of preparation. Brooks believes that both devices are "duplicators" rather than "copiers," based on the arbitrary numerical criterion that more than 10 to 20 copies are duplicates.(19) The market place became more in need of an efficient, fast, and economical copier that did not require the making of a master page. During the 1930s and 1940s two new copiers were marketed: the Photostat (a paper negative or positive copying process) and the Recordak (a microfilming system).

In the two decades following the 1940s several useful methods of photocopying documents were introduced. These new processes can be grouped under six categories: (a) diffusion transfer, (b) physical transfer, (c) quick stabilization, (d) Diazo, (e) thermography, and (f) electrostatography.(20) Almost all of these found a ready market, partly because they satisfied a need and partly because they exercised a powerful psychological fascination on their users. "In a society that sociologists are forever characterizing as 'mass' the notion of making one-of-a-kind things showed signs of becoming a real compulsion."(21) The use of these devices was no longer restricted to the business world. They won over every possible field, from police departments using copies to produce pictographic receipts for property removed from prisoners to hospitals copying electrocardiograms and laboratory reports. In fact, anybody with any need for a copy can go to many stores that have a coin-operated machine and make as many copies as he deems necessary as long as he feeds the machine with the required coins. It is interesting to note that the "Xerox Corporation [for example] produces coin-operated 914s in two configurations – one that works for a dime and one that works for a quarter – the buyer or leaser of the machine decides what he wants to charge."(22) By the 1950s the market was flooded by several devices capable of reproducing almost any document at a cost of only a few cents per copy and within a space of a minute or less per copy.

As a general term to include all the variations in techniques and methods of copying, a new word, "reprography" (derived from "reproduction" and the familiar Greek root for writing, "graph") was coined around the end of the 1950s. Reprography (German "Reprographic") became a label first in the United Kingdom and Germany.(23) The term gained international recognition at the First International Congress of Reprography, which was held in Cologne, Germany, in October 1963.(24) The term "reprography" is difficult to define. Ibrahim defines it as a "technology of producing and reproducing visual communications in an in-plant operation." In elaboration, she continues:

> Reprography groups all the techniques used for reproducing, duplicating, storing and retrieving visually recorded messages in a sphere usually called office and administrative. Specifically, reprography includes all small format printing, multicopying and duplicating techniques, notably electrophotography, xerography, diffusion transfer, thermography, offset lithography, mimeography, Diazo methods, microfilming, and other data storage and retrieval systems.(25)

Scientists and scholars always felt free to copy by hand the work of others for their own research and use. When copiers became available and common, it was a "simple transition" for the scholar to extend his notetaking to photocopying. Publishers had accepted longhand copying because of its physical limitations. The publishers' objection is based on quick and easy copying which, if allowed to increase, it is claimed, will affect the market for research material to the point where publication will be self-defeating. Eventually, the publishers claim, there will be nothing left for scholars to photocopy.(26)

A primary need of present-day society is accessibility to information. Traditional library service provided access by permitting the perusal (and copying) of the original document in the library. Lending privileges were extended first with multiple copies and later with any copy of certain books, but even in the most liberal libraries loans have rarely extended to heavily used reference books or to the bound copies of periodicals.(27)

According to the last census, the population of the United States is more than 200 million. It has been estimated that 25% of the population are registered borrowers who use public libraries where books for home use are stocked in quantity. Library users have not only increased in number, but have also experienced a "radical change in age distribution and a vast churning across the land."(28)

Today's users are more educated than their predecessors, and we are becoming a society of specialists. The body of knowledge to be made available through libraries has also been transformed with equal rapidity. Until a century ago "the growth of most library collections was largely the fruit of individual munifence," (29) and the increase of knowledge was propelled by the

curiosity of individuals.   By the beginning of the 20th
century research began to play a major role in our
lives.   An explosion of information took place during
and after World War II.   Government and voluntary
groups devoted enormous sums of money to scientific
research and technical development.   Lacy stated that

> an average annual investment for these purposes
> [in the postwar decade] was 15 billion dollars.
> This was more than the entire gross national
> product of all but a few nations and more
> than that of the United States itself only a
> few decades before....   One consequence was
> an enormous and rapid increase in the amount
> of recorded information produced, especially in
> the fields of physical and biological sciences,
> engineering and medicine.   The number of
> books published in these fields increased from
> 1,576 in 1940 to 4,933 in 1965; the number
> of journals rose proportionately.(30)

The problem was also complicated by thousands of
unpublished scientific reports.   There was no doubt
that the scholar and the library had to face a flood
of material revolutionary in its volume and complexity
at a time when access to information was considered
an obligation of society and its agency, the library.
The only way to cope with the situation was through
the development of new technologies in recording, storing,
retrieving, and producing documents.   Photocopying,
among other devices, became an essential part of the
library operation and an integral part of the information
industry as a unit operation.   The practice became so
common and was welcomed to the extent that the
American Library Association established a Copying
Methods Section.   By 1959 the section found it
necessary to publish the *Directory of Institutional
Photoduplication Services in the United States.*   Since
the demand was great and the number of library

photoduplication services had considerably increased, a second, revised edition was published in 1962, followed by updated editions in July 1966 and in 1973, and was further expanded to include library photocopying services located anywhere in the world.(31)

Photocoping practice was so commonplace that in 1962 it was estimated that about 3.6 billion copies were made annually.(32)   In 1967, 27.5 billion paper copies were produced.(33)   The increase was accelerated by the declining cost of photocopying from twenty-five cents per copy to one-half cent per page.(34)   For example, in April 1970, the Xerox Corporation announced that its Model 914 produced seven copies per minute at a cost of five cents per copy; Model 813 (which is a table-top model) produces 11 copies per minute for four cents a copy; the 660 model produces 11 copies per minute for four and one-half cents per copy; the 720 model makes 12 copies per minute for three cents per copy; the 3600 produces 1 to 20 copies for nine-tenths of one cent and 20 to 40 copies for a cheaper rate; and the 7000 model makes copies for as little as twenty-one-tenths of one cent per copy.(35)   What the future will bring in the development of faster and less expensive copy machines remains to be seen.   But if it continues at the rate that has been observed for the last 15 years, one can assume that the cost for copying will be a virtually negligible consideration on the part of users and libraries alike.

Many studies have been conducted to examine the problem, and several reports have been published.   The report of the Committee to Investigate Copyright Problems (CICP) could be considered representative of the findings of the other studies.   The CICP study, which was sponsored by the U.S. Office of Education, surveyed six libraries during March 1967 and found that the number of publishers whose works were copied in

these libraries were as follows: Bowdoin, 60; Fort
Detrick, 93; Harvard, 158; John Crerar, 482; Lockheed,
142; and Stanford Law, 25. The survey also found
that the total number of pages of books copied that
month in these libraries was 31,000 and the total
materials in page numbers copied in the same libraries
during the same month was 43,000. However, the
ratio of journal copies to book copies was 9 to 1,(36)
and 41 to 100 percent of all items copied were scientific or technical. The study also determined that 80
percent of the material copied was less than five years
old and that "the number of multiple copies of the
same document made for the same client by U.S. libraries is almost negligible." On the other hand, the
study found that the copying of nonprofit, noncommercial journals dominated the copying of commercial
journals by 2 to 1; this was reversed in books by a
ratio of 1 to 2. It was also found that journal
articles were almost always copied in toto and that
books were copied only in part.

Other surveys and several published opinions have
voiced the publishers' (commercial or noncommercial)
concerns over current copying practices with respect to
their copyrighted journals. Publishers indicate that they
suffer potential damages through(37) (1) loss of sales and
subscriptions; (2) declining sales of back issues and reprints; and (3) loss of advertising revenues.

A.   Loss of Sales and Subscriptions

Many publishers and readers alike agree that the
price of scientific books has risen sharply in recent
years. The case can be documented retrospectively as
follows:(38)

Year of publication	Price per page
1957	2.5 cents
1967	3.8 cents
1972	6.1 cents

Thus, prices have increased 144 percent over a 15-year period, and about 60 percent of that increase has occurred in the last five years. Benjamin warned that one should not assume that publishers are getting rich on sales at current high prices, because the contrary is true. Publication of books is becoming less profitable as sales continue to decline due to rising prices. Consequently, many publishers have felt compelled to cut down on production, and as a result editions are becoming smaller in quantity, resulting in a proportionately higher cost per unit produced with a concomitant decrease in sales. This can be seen clearly when the index of sales per title in the five-year period of publication is compared in the same three aforementioned years:(39)

Year[*]	Copies sold
1957	4,977
1967	3,761
1972	2,961

The buyer's resistance to higher prices is a major factor in the increase of book prices. Rising costs, however, have made higher prices inevitable. Increased costs of labor and paper and higher postal rates are some of the production costs that are considered by the publisher when he sets the price of the final product.

*Years indicate the end of the five year sales period.

The publishing industry, as the sixth largest industry in the United States in terms of income,(40) has come to realize that libraries and librarians constitute the most predictable of their clientele. Libraries are something like a captive market for the published word and a primary contributor to its continuation. With economic problems that are reflected in the decrease of operating budgets, libraries buy fewer books and journals and become more selective in what they purchase.

Another factor is the "twigging phenomenon," particularly in the publication of scientific works. Benjamin describes the phenomenon as

> the fractionation of scientific knowledge and hence of the subject matter of scientific books ... this endless fractionation results in scores of highly specialized books being written each year for groups of readers that are no larger today than they were 25 years ago, despite the fact that our population of scientists has more than quadrupled in the past quarter of a century.(41)

Although the tree is getting bigger every year and general scientific books are sold in much larger numbers, the market for the twig books, the specialized and advanced treatises, has not increased at all. Since the price of a new book is determined by dividing the total cost by the number of copies printed, one can understand the result of spreading the every-increasing "plant" costs over a constant number of copies printed for the last 25 years.

Any suggestions of applying and using the new technological advances to cut down the costs of composition and printing on short-term editions proved to be futile. There is no doubt that there are accrued savings but they are not enough to offset the increase in other elements of operating costs. In this respect, Benjamin noted:

> Production cost of the average monograph is
> usually no more than 25 percent of the list
> price.   (A typical formula for pricing a pre-
> sumably profitable monograph covers other
> costs — discounts, royalty, advertising and sales,
> order fulfillment and general overhead.)   That
> typically amounts to about 67 percent of the
> list price.   This leaves the publisher some 8
> percent for operating profit before taxes at the
> 54 percent corporate rate — but, of course,
> neither the typical formula nor the tax charge
> can be applied to the monograph that does
> not sell well enough to cover the cost of its
> first printing.(42)

The matter is more complicated because there is no way
of knowing in advance if a publication will sell.   While
other industries can test a product on the market,
publishers have no way of doing that until after the
fact.

Studies have shown, however, that, compared to
journals, books are rarely copied.   Journal publishers
seem to have more reason to believe that photocopying
will affect their business.

As some publishers put it, the unprecedented
technological progress of the last decade harms the
environment the way DDT affects wildlife, and if the
condition is permitted to continue it may go beyond
the point of no return.(43)   One may say that the
purpose of photocopying is to help the dissemination
of scientific information.   Uncontrolled, however,
photocopying may destroy the incentive for writing and
the economic viability in publication.   Publishers of
scientific periodicals are at the high end of the spectrum
of those who are badly hurt by photocopying.   The
reason for this, as the president of Williams & Wilkins
Company claims, is that a scientist will go to the
library, examine the tables of contents of the journals
in his field, and acquire a photocopy of the articles

that interest him.   In doing so, the scientist is substituting a photocopy for a subscription or a reprint from
the author, to say the least.(44)

The extent of photocopying scientific journals is
sizable.   Under the Fair Disclosure Act, the Williams &
Wilkins Company was able to examine the records of
the National Institutes of Health and the National Library of Medicine and prove that 1 million pages of the
journals published by the company were photocopied by
200 medical libraries during 1968.   There is no doubt
that photocopying of this magnitude has an effect on
the economics of journal publishing.

The problem is compounded by the now accepted
concept of resource sharing whereby only one subscription of a given periodical is needed and all other libraries in the system share in it by obtaining photocopies of portions as needed.   Since library subscriptions to journals are important, particularly to those
which have a relatively low circulation, the extent of
damage may be significant.   For instance, a drop of
400 subscriptions to a journal which sells for $40
a year and has 4000 subscribers could mean an
increase of $4 per subscription to offset the loss of
subscribers.   This effect would be more damaging if
the journal had fewer subscribers to start with.   The
general feeling of commercial publishers, therefore, is
that the "burgeoning phenomenon of machine reproduction" has begun to force scientific journals out of
existence.(45)

A survey of 21 journals published by the Williams
& Wilkins Company indicated a steady rise in subscriptions until 1965.   A decline followed in 1965 to
1967 which was attributed by the company primarily
to the increase in photocopying.(46)

Scientific journals are also published by scientific
societies for the purpose of disseminating scientific

knowledge rather than for profit. However, nonprofit publishers must break even if they are to continue publication without subsidy. Since the majority of them do not accept, or are not supported by, advertising they have to rely solely on subscriptions. Another means of support is the government funding mechanism in whole or in part to these publications. This support takes several forms:

1. A grant of public funds to an individual in in response to a research proposal

2. A contract to an institution to conduct research

3. Page charges paid out of federal funds to journals

4. Grants or contracts for publication and/or distribution of journals

In 1973 this type of support amounted to $7,815,000. (47) For that reason, many federal agencies have protected their right to copy free of charge any publications resulting from research or activities subsidized by them. The reason is that the government has paid for the original research and usually subsidizes the publication emanating from it to ensure its existence and facilitate its circulation. For example, one policy regarding the public health service states:

> Except as may otherwise be provided under the terms and conditions of the award, the grantee may copyright ... any publication ... developed or resulting from research projects supported by a grant under this part, subject, however, to a royalty-free nonexclusive license or right in the Government to reproduce, translate, publish, use, disseminate and dispose of such material and to authorize others to do so.(48)

The publisher in these cases does not encumber his budget with any expense for acquiring the article or securing the ready-to-print pages.   In addition, he is not under any obligation to pay royalties to the author at any time.   This type of publisher can, therefore, determine his cost and accordingly the number of copies to be printed and the subscription rate in order for him to cover this cost and make a reasonable gain.

Nonprofit publishers, however, also complain about photocopying and give many examples of mass photosuplication of their publications (for example, the deputy director of the National Library of Medicine admitting that the library supplies medical libraries with copies at the rate of 2 million pages per year).(49)

Copying machines are also installed and used in business stores and, in some instances, constitutes a sideline to the store's normal line of business.   The *Wall Street Journal* quotes the president of a men's clothing store in Cambridge, Massachusetts, where the biggest and fastest copying machine is next to the necktie counter, as stating that the machine is steadily used nine hours a day by students from Harvard University who "dash in and Xerox chapters of books in short supply at the library, or articles from scholarly journals that they have smuggled out."(50)   The president admitted that the store is planning to install a second machine.

B.   Declining Sales of Back Issues and Reprints

Publishers also claim that they suffer potential damage because of diminishing sales of back issues and reprints.   Libraries would rather make copies of journals they do not have in their collections, which they acquire through interlibrary loans, than buy a back issue or a reprint of the article needed.   This claim, however,

assumes the availability of the back issue at the publisher's warehouse and the easy acquisition of the needed
offprints from him or from the author of the article.
This assumption is not true all the time, as publishers
do not usually stock back issues in quantities to meet
future demands and consider offprints as a "reader
service" rendered for no profit.   Publishers of scientific
journals are not interested and not really prepared to
supply such copies or reprints.   The logistics and the
expense of storing, plus the monies tied up in reprints
and back issues for which demand cannot be predicted,
are too prohibitive for publishers to pursue this kind of
service seriously.   Marke stated, for example, that he
wrote to about 2,000 publishers for permission to reproduce certain publications for an annotated catalog and
in reply heard from only 50 publishers.   "Most never
replied, many of the authors had died, some publishers
had gone out of business; [and] in many cases, there
was nobody to reply."(51)   The question is, What
should the library or the user do if there is a need
for a certain publication that is not available at its
source?   Are libraries and users entitled to make copies
of nonavailable material because of an unanswered or
denied request?   And if the publisher or the author
grants the permission is he entitled to collect
licensing fees?

C.   Loss of Advertising Revenues

In addition to the above-mentioned claims, publishers
express fears of the dilution of advertising revenues.
Advertisement is dependent on the volume of sales:
the wider the circulation the more appealing the journal
is for advertisement, as many readers will see it.   A
decline in the number of subscriptions may result, therefore, in reduced spending by advertisers in a given

journal.   In addition, the trend in copying is to avoid reproducing pages that contain nothing but advertisement, which results in eliminating the advertisement altogether from the used copy.   In the meantime, the cost of advertising is based on guaranteed circulation and is strictly controlled by the provisions of the Audit Bureau of Circulation.   The greater the proven circulation from the sale of newstand copies and from subscriptions, the higher the price to the advertiser.   Periodicals must publish a true analysis of circulation and heavy penalties may be imposed for false statements.

Publishers also discovered that the core of their subscription list was made up of libraries which were amazingly compliant and continued their subscriptions even as the price was raised to double the original amount.   However, budgetary pressures have made libraries review their subscriptions and seek other methods, such as resource sharing, to prevent serious financial problems.   Resource sharing among libraries could amount to a vast reduction in the number of subscriptions and could bring an end to the financial security that libraries' subscriptions have heretofore represented.   Libraries have in effect supported advertising revenues, so that the loss of library subscriptions will have an even more drastic effect by both reducing the expected revenue from subscribers and preventing an increase in revenue from advertising.

NOTES

1. Charles F. Gosnell, "The Copying Grap Bag: Observation on the New Copyright Legislation." *ALA
   BULLETIN* 60: 46-47 (Jan. 1966).

2. John Clement Harrison, "History." In *Copyright:
   Current Viewpoints on History, Laws, Legislation.*
   edited by A. Kent and H. Lancour. New York:
   Bowker, 1971, p. 1.

3. Cambridge Research Institute, *Omnibus Copyright Revision: Cooperative Analysis of the Issues.*
   Washington, D. C.: American Society for Information Science, 1973.

4. Harrison, *op. cit.*

5. United States Constitution, Article 1, Section 8.

6. Copyright Law of the United States of America, United
   States Code, Title 17; Copyright Revised to January
   1, 1973, Circular 91. Washington, D. C.: Copyright Office.

7. Julius J. Marke, "Copyright Revisited." *Wilson Library
   Bulletin* 42: 37 (Sept. 1967).

8. Douglas N. Mount, "Copyright: The Situation Now."
   Publishers Weekly 199: 25-27 (July 5, 1971).

9. Julius J. Marke, *Copyright and Intellectual Property.*
   New York: Fund for the Advancement of Education, 1967, p. 72.

10. *Encyclopedia International*, 1974, Vol. 10, p. 514.

11. Daniel Lacy, "Social Changes and the Library: 1947-
    1980." In *Libraries at Large,* edited by Douglas
    M. Knight and E. Shipley Nourse, New York:
    Bowker, 1969. p. 21.

12. Eric Moon, "Satisfaction Point." *Library Journal*
    93: 1947 (May 15, 1968).

13. S. Rothstein, "Library Services to Users." *Encyclo-
    pedia American*, Intern. edi. 1973, Vol. 17,
    p. 374.

14. *Oxford English Dictionary.* Oxford: Clarendon Press, 1933, Vol. 11, pp. 978-979.

15. *Black's Law Dictionary,* 6th ed. St. Paul: West, 1951, p. 405.

16. John Brooks, "Profiles: xerox xerox xerox xerox." *The New Yorker* 63: 46 (April 1, 1967).

17. *Ibid.*

18. *Ibid.*

19. *Ibid.*

20. Glenn E. Matthews, "Photocopying." *Encyclopedia Americana.* New York: Americana Corp., 1973, Vol. 22, p. 11g

21. Brooks, *op. cit.,* p. 47.

22. *Ibid.,* p. 58.

23. George P. Bush, ed, *Technology and Copyright.* Mt. Airy, Md.: Lomond Systems Inc., 1971, p. 24.

24. Karen Ibrahim, "Exploring the Meaning of 'Reprography.' " *Graphic Arts Progress* 16: 10 (1969).

25. *Ibid.,* pp. 10-12.

26. Marke, *op. cit.,* p. 73.

27. Carl Overhage. "Plans for Project Intrex." *Science* 152: 1032 (May 20, 1966).

28. Lacy, *op. cit.,* p. 5.

29. Joseph C. Shipman, "Collection Building." *Encyclopedia of Library and Information Science.* New York: Marcel Dekker, 1971, p. 260.

30. Lacy, *op. cit.,* p. 6.

31. Cosby Brinkley, *Directory of Library Photoduplication Services.* Chicago: American Library Association, 1966, p. 1.

32. J. C. Koepke, "Assessment of Documentation Practices in Reprography." *Reprography and Copyright Law.* Lowell H. Hattery, ed. Washington, D. C.: American Institute of Biological Sciences, 1964, p. 51.

33. John H. Dessauer, *Establish a Select Senate Committee on Technology and the Human Environment.* Washington, D. C.: Government Printing Office, 1969, p. 150.

34. Nicholas L. Henry, "Copyright, Public Policy and Information Technology." *Science* 183: 387 (Feb. 1, 1974).

35. Irwin Karp. "Copyright – the Author's View." In *Copyright – the Librarian and the Law,* edited by George Lukac, pp. 45-46. New Brunswick, N. J.: Rutgers University Graduate School of Library Service, 1972.

36. Gerald J. Sophar and Lawrance B. Heilprin, *The Determination of Legal Facts and Economic Guideposts with Respect to the Dissemination of Scientific and Educational Information as it is Affected by Copyright – A Status Report.* Washington, D. C.: Bureau of Research, Office of Education, Department of Health, Education and Welfare, p. 23.

37. *Survey of Copyrighted Material Reproduction Practices in Scientific and Technical Fields.* Chicago: George Fry & Associates, 1961, p. ii.

38. Benjamin, *op. cit.,* p. 282.

39. *Ibid.*

40. Johanna Elenore Tallman, "Opinion Paper: An Affirmative Statement on Copyright Debate." *Journal of the American Society for Information Science* 25: 147 (May-June 1974).

41. Benjamin, *op. cit.,* p. 283.

42. *Ibid.,* p. 284.

43. William M. Passano, "How Photocopying Pollutes Sci-Tech Publishing." *Publishers Weekly* 197: 63 (Feb. 2, 1970).

44. *Ibid.*

45. J. H. Kuney, "A Publisher's Viewpoint – Not for Profit."
    In *Copyright: Current Viewpoints on History, Laws,
    Legislation.* A. Kent and H. Lancour, eds. New
    York: Bowker, 1971, p. 54.

46. S. Allen, "New Technology and the Law of Copyright."
    UCLA Law Review 15: 944 (April 1968).

47. *Federal Funds for Research, Development, and other
    Scientific Activities, Fiscal Year 1971, 1972 and
    1973.* Washington, D. C.: National Science Founda-
    tion, 1971, pp. 42, 194.

48. Code of Federal Regulation, Title 42 – Public Health,
    revised as of October 1, 1972, Part 52-53, p. 118.

49. Allen, *op. cit.,* p. 943.

50. *Ibid.,* p. 1

51. Julius Marke, "The Copyright Controversy: Issues and
    Opinions: The Group Discussion." *Drexel Library
    Quarterly* 8: 404 (Oct. 1972).

Chapter 2

TRENDS IN COPYING

One may ask whether photoduplication of copyrighted material really is a widespread practice. The answer is an unequivocal "yes," and the practice is growing rapidly.(1)

It is almost impossible to estimate the actual number of photocopies of copyrighted material now produced annually. However, in 1962 the Xerox Corporation estimated that 300 million photocopies of all types of material were produced *each month* in the United States.(2) Since then, the figure has grown astronomically and continues to grow every day. A quantitative estimate of photocopying of copyrighted material is hazardous for several reasons: (a) Not all copied material is copyrighted (much is in the public domain, such as government publications; (b) there are thousands of copying machines in universities, colleges, public libraries, schools of all kinds, offices, churches, businesses, hospitals, and almost everywhere else; and (c) the logistics of getting a count of every copy made by every copying machine is beyond human ability. The effect of photocopying, however, would not be determined by a quantitative analysis, in any case.

Photocopying is practiced in information centers as an integral part of their operation and services. There are differences, however, in this practice of copying, which can be put into four categories: (a) single copies, (b) multiple copies, (c) part of work, and (d) whole work.

25

A.   Single Copies

This practice is common in public and government
libraries.   The photocopying in this category is done in
response to a request for a single copy.   These types of
libraries will make a single copy of any particular item for
one individual.   This is also true if the same individual
asks for a single copy of more than one item.   The key
to the parctice is the "single copy."   The majority of
these libraries have strict rules prohibiting multiple copying
and in practice "will not knowingly provide multiple copies
to the same individual."(3)   The rule applies to the copying done by the library for its clientele.   Despite the
printed notices on many copying machines installed in
libraries there is no way of ascertaining that the "single-
copy rule" is followed when the client himself is making
the copies on the coin-operated machines provided on the
premises of public and academic libraries.   Special libraries, however, exercise a certain amount of control
because copying is a free service offered to a restricted
number of users.

B.   Multiple Copies

This practice is largely done in college and university libraries and in information centers.   It is true that
college and university libraries perform a single-copy service,
not only for students and faculty, but also for outsiders,
and some of it is done in lieu of an interlibrary loan of
the actual material.   These libraries, however, are known
to produce multiple copies of material mainly for their
own internal reserve use, either to meet the requests of
faculty members or to supplement their collections with
multiple copies of frequently used works or those much
in demand at certain points in the school year.

The reprographic practice in these libraries is either partial reproduction of any work, or total reproduction of the complete work.

C. Partial Reproduction

Partial reproduction is done in response to requests for copies of certain parts of a book (for example, chapters, pages, tables, or appendixes) or part of an article from a journal that contains several articles. This type of copying is done mainly by or for an individual, as when the library offers the service in response to a faculty or a researcher's request. This partial reproduction could be done in multiple copies as well as on a single-copy basis.

D. Total Work Reproduction

Total work reproduction is mainly a library practice and is usually a result of a need to provide for certain courses with large numbers of students who must use the same work at the same time. Complete articles from scientific journals and short out-of-print books no longer available are most often copied. A careful librarian usually makes sure that the work is not available in paperbacks or in reprints before reproducing it. Textbooks, however, are not a target of this kind of practice, as instructors usually do not assign out-of-print textbooks for class reading. On the other hand, libraries may make copies to preserve an expensive and irreplaceable original work. Publishers of these works state that reproduction of total work is a clear and obvious case of violation of their copyright, particularly when it is done in multiple copies that would otherwise appear as a need to reprint.
  Much of the material needed for library collections and research in recent years in copyrighted. The question is whether making and providing photocopies of copyrighted

material without permission of the copyright owner is a violation of his right according to Section 1(a) of the copyright law. Section 1 of the copyright law provides among other rights that the copyright owner shall have the exclusive right to print, reprint, publish, copy, and vend the copyrighted work.

The law, therefore, is clear about the copyright owner's exclusive right to reprint or copy his work, whether by himself or by another with his permission. The law does not impose any limitations on the copyright owner's exclusive right to copy. This means that an individual or institution cannot reproduce by any means or method a page, a part, or a total work without the permission of the copyright owner. Society, through the law, grants such exclusive control to the owner in the belief that it is necessary to encourage authorship and scholarship. The only exception is the Fair Use Doctrine developed by courts through judicial interpretation which further evolved through cooperative efforts between librarians and publishers. Judges Learned Hand, August Hand, and Robert Patterson stated in a *per curiam* opinion that "the issue of fair use ... is the most troublesome in the whole law of copyright...."(4) The problem emanated partly from the fact that the U.S. copyright act did not provide for or define fair use. Case law has developed certain standards that apply, but the facts relating to the case in litigation determine the outcome. Fair use is a rule in equity cases and is redefined as each of the facts in each case are determined. If a definition has to be attempted, Pforzheimer defines fair use as

> the use without copyright owner's consent
> of such portion of a copyrighted publication as
> a copyright proprietor might reasonable expect
> might be so utilized, given the type and nature
> of the publication in question; and would not be
> such a qualitative taking as to constitute an in-
> fringement within normal judicial concepts of the term.(5)

Historically, the doctrine was first discussed in 1841 by Justice Story in *Folson* v. *March* when he wrote:

> ... we must often, in deciding questions of this sort, look to the nature and objects of the selection made, the quantity and value of the material used and the degree in which the use may prejudice the sale or diminish the profits or supersede the objects of the original work.(6)

This court decision indicates that the major criteria as to what constitutes fair use are (a) the purpose for which the copy is taken, (b) the nature of the copyrighted work, (c) the size and importance of the copy in relation to the copyrighted work, and (d) the effect of the use of the copy on the demand for the copyrighted work.

Fair use has to be viewed not as a permission to copy but as an exception to the exclusive right of the owner. This leads to the question of what fair use is, and what is unfair or an infringement of copyright. From a strictly practical viewpoint, copyright may be considered as the "right to sell multiple copies and to profit thereby."(7) The difference between fair use and infringement, therefore, is a matter of the purpose, degree, and the effect of copying rather than the act of copying itself. The differentiation between fair use and infringement is fundamentally a problem of balancing what the author must allow in return for his exclusive statutory copyright. No court can arbitrarily state general measurements as to what could be considered fair use or otherwise that could be applied in every situation. Although precise measurements cannot be incorporated in a statute, the statute should nevertheless recognize the concept of fair use while leaving its interpretation to the courts.*

---

*This recommendation is now included in Chapter III, Copyright Law Revision.

The fact is that the 1909 act is silent on the question of fair use and the 1947 amendments do not mention the doctrine. One provision, however, had an indirect impact on the issue. Section 1 (b) extends to the owner of a copyright in literary work the exclusive right "to make any version thereof." This was in contradiction to prior case law, under which a "bona fide abridgement" was permissible. In general, however, the criteria for and application of fair use are discernible in a body of case law unaffected by legislative development.

There are two ways of looking at fair use: (a) as an infringement which is nevertheless excused (privileged infringement) or (b) as the use of copyrighted material that does not fall within the domain of the copyright protection, which is therefore not considered an infringement (negated infringement). One theory behind this kind of permissible copying is the "implied consent of the copyright owner."(8) This theory is debatable in light of statements requiring written consent for any quotations (that is, "All rights reserved. No part of this book/publication may be used or reproduced without written permission...."). Latman theorizes, however, that as a condition of obtaining the statutory protection, the author has supposedly consented to certain reasonable uses of his copyrighted work to promote knowledge in the interest of the public.(9) This approach is consistent with the general assumption that fair use does not apply to common law literary property of unpublished works.(10)

Fair use is seen in a wide range of situations reflecting, in essence, the basic conflict between the copyright owner's insistence on his exclusive right and the user's conviction that his use does not infringe on

such right.   This study is concerned, however, with the
case of personal or private use.   Shaw argued that
"private use is completely outside the scope and intent
of restrictions by copyright."(11)   Since until recently
there was no litigation, one could assume that the
copyright owner does not object to that kind of use.
However, this does not seem to be absolutely true
since there have been several attempts to regulate the
role of libraries in supplying copies from copyrighted
works to their users, such as the Gentleman's Agreement.

E.   Gentlemen's Agreement

As previously mentioned, the copyright law as it
stands is silent about fair use.   This created a deep
concern among scholars, scientists, researchers, and librarians regarding their fair utilization of copyrighted
research material.   This was further complicated by the
rapid advancement of photocopying technology, which
introduced the possibility of reproducing research material
in quantity inexpensively.   The question, however, was
whether the copyright law was applicable to the library
practice of reproducing such copies of parts of a book
or a single article from a journal for its clientele's
private use.   In this respect Shaw stated:

> No cases have ever been brought into court.
> Fair use has never referred to the making of a
> single copy by a scholar, or lawyer, or author,
> or anyone else for his own use.   The term as
> an incident of literary property, appears to apply
> solely to production and/or sale of multiple copies
> or what has the same effect, the presentation to
> a group of people....   The making of such single
> copies, for private use, was never in the minds

> of those who developed the common law or the
> statute and such use of literary property is not
> affected by either.   It violates no law at all
> and is a right of scholars.(12)

At the other extreme is the writer who viewed such
copying as that which "would constitute an infringement
in principle at least ... if an individual made copies for
personal use, even in his own handwriting...."(13)
Shallenberg, however, took a middle of the road position,
claiming "that Shaw went too far in assuming that the
Federal copyright statute was not intended to interfere
with the production of single copies."(14)

The deep concern of scholars, librarians, and publishers led to the development of the Gentleman's Agreement.
The credit for that development goes to the Joint Committee on Materials for Research, which was organized
around 1930 through the joint efforts of the American
Council of Learned Societies and the Social Science
Research Council.(15)   It consisted of scholars, librarians,
and museologists who, through coorespondence, contacted
interested parties and obtained information regarding
photocopying and research material.   By 1934 Robert
Brinkley, chairman of the joint committee, wrote a
memorandum on the problem of copyright law as it
relates to research material for distribution among the
joint committee and sent a copy of it to Frederic
Melcher, chairman of the Committee on Copyright in
the National Association of Book Publishers, soliciting
his comments.(16)   The problem of photocopying in
all its facets was covered as it affected researchers and
librarians acting for their clientele in the replacement
of worn, stolen, lost, or unavailable material, or for
filling interlibrary loan requests, or as substitutes for
loans.   Melcher's response indicated that it should be
permissible for a scholar or a library to photocopy
scattered paragraphs from a copyrighted work.   In his

opinion, however, copying of a whole work, be it a book or an article in a journal, constitutes an infringement, whether the copy was made by the researcher or by a library.   He further stated:

> It should be noted that because a book is out of print the rights to copy do not cease.   In fact, the best chance for there being a new edition is to have all the demands for a new printing concentrated in responsible hands.(17)

As a result, the joint committee decided to negotiate an agreement with the National Association of Book Publishers, which has since gone out of existence. Through meetings and deliberations a code of fair practice, better known as the Gentleman's Agreement, was worked out to protect the rights of both the copyright owner and the scholar.

In brief, the Agreement assigns responsibilities and prescribes that librarians obtain a written "order" for a single photocopy of any published work or any part of it for research purposes with dangers of infringement clearly delineated.   The "order" makes this also clear to the person who requests the copy.   The agreement was later made the basis of a Material Production Code, prepared by the Association of Research Libraries, and was adopted in 1940 by the American Library Association.

The agreement and the code helped to improve the relationship between libraries and publishers.   However, new developments in copying technology and new trends in copying practices led to further discussions that in 1957 resulted in the establishment of a Joint Library Committee on Fair Use in Photocopying, which consisted of representatives from the four major professional library associations.   The joint committee used the fair use doctrine as a basis for a set of rules

that became a part of the American Library Association
Copyright Issue Committee's report in January 1964.   The
findings of the report were as follows:

1. The making of a single copy by a library is a
   direct and natural extension of traditional library
   service.

2. Such service, employing modern copying methods,
   has become essential.

3. The present demand can be satisfied without in-
   flicting measurable damage on publishers and
   copyright owners.

4. Improved copying processes will not materially
   affect the demand for single-copy library duplication for research purpose.(18)

These rules and the validity of the Gentleman's
Agreement were put to the test in the U.S. Court of
Claims in the case of *Williams & Wilkins Company* v.
*National Institutes of Health and National Library of
Medicine,* which will be discussed at length in Chapter
4.   Briefly, the Gentleman's Agreement was considered
no longer valid because a signator no longer existed and
in any case the agreement did not support the defendant's copying practices.

The commissioner's opinion in the case was in favor
of the publisher, and the case has since gone to higher
courts for appeal.   The question is, What should libraries do now: stop all photocopying or enter into
royalty agreements with the copyright owners?   To
explore these questions, representatives of a number of
libraries and other associations met in Washington D. C.,
on 24 February 1972.   The organizations represented:

American Association of Junior Colleges

American Association of Law Libraries

American Association of Law Schools

American Library Association

Association of Research Libraries

Joint Council on Educational Telecommunications

National Library of Medicine

Special Libraries Associations

It was agreed that, "until a final decision is reached in the Williams & Wilkins case, it is desirable that the library world should continue existing policies and practices with respect to photocopying of copyrighted materials...."(19)   Subsequently, the case was decided by the full bench of the court of claims in favor of the libraries and this decision was then appealed to the U.S. Supreme Court, which, in essence, upheld the decision.

F.   Interlibrary Loans and Resource Sharing

Man is fulfilled as he shares in and enriches his cultural heritage.   His survival, his self-realization and his social enlightenment turn upon his knowledge of the concepts, habits, skills, arts, instruments and institutions of that heritage.   In advanced societies his knowledge of that heritage depends increasingly upon recorded information resources.   To these resources every man, according to his needs, should have realistic access.

The tremendous growth and diversification of this information resource in modern times are abundantly evident....   The resource having outreached the capacity of any man, or of all men, to learn and

remember, the issue of its preservation and
effective use has become critical.(20)

It is a fact that no one library and no one type
of library can be self-sufficient in serving its users.
Statements of standards and objectives by major types of
library division in the American Library Association specify
the importance of interlibrary cooperation.

Verner Clapp, in presenting the Eighteenth Windsor
Lecture in Librarianship for 1963 at the University of
Illinois, noted that self-sufficiency requires all materials
needed for research to be immediately at hand.(21)
We have to differentiate in this respect between physical
and bibliographic self-sufficiency. Physical self-sufficiency
is the ability of the library to provide its users with
requested information from its own collection. On the
other hand, bibliographic self-sufficiency is the ability
of the library to provide its users with bibliographic
and local identification of one or more citations of
research materials.(22) Today, the impossibility of both
concepts is obvious. The basic concepts of librarianship
are to acquire, organize, and disseminate information upon
demand. However, certain factors emerged in the last
two decades which make it rather difficult for any given
library to function effectively on its own within the
aforementioned concepts. The changes in American
education and culture have resulted in increasing and
accelerating reader demands upon libraries. The changes
in quantity and variety of published materials make it
impossible for any given library to acquire every published work. This is coupled with the rising costs of
materials, equipment, and service, which at today's
standards are beyond the reach of any single library.(23)

Libraries, however, attempt to achieve self-sufficiency.
One of the supporting factors is the development in
photocopying technology which makes it possible for a
library to acquire from other libraries a copy of a

missing item to supplement its own collection. The most pressing factor, however, is the demand of users. Most users are concerned with the immediate access of materials rather than with cooperation. Librarians are constantly pressured to keep in house those materials that are in demand. Full ownership of library materials combined with institutional pride leads some to believe that cooperation is fine in theory but not in practice.(24)

Libraries are frequently regarded as "bottomless pits," and it is not likely in our present period of inflation that those in control of financial resources will constantly increase library budgets from one year to the next for the sake of self-sufficiency. Tough financial times reinforce the need for cooperation.(25)

The number of new books and periodicals is increasing at an exponential rate. Between 1940 and 1960, ten large American libraries increased their acquisitions by 71 percent to cope with the flood of material. DeSola Price indicated that scientific journals have increased from 10 journals in 1600 to about 100 in 1800, then to 10,000 in 1900, and finally to almost 100,000 in 1960. He also indicated that the number of scientific periodicals doubles every 15 years, a pattern that has been maintained for the last three centuries.(26)

Interlibrary loans as an approach to better service was first mentioned in the first issue of *Library Journal* in September 1876. In a letter to the editor dated 4 September 1876, Samuel Swett Green, librarian of the Worcester Free Public Library, wrote:

> It would add greatly to the usefulness of our reference libraries if an agreement should be made to lend books to each other for short periods of time. It happens not infrequently that some book is called for by a reader, or that in looking up the answer to a question a

> librarian has occasion to use a book which he
> finds in the catalog of another library, but
> which does not belong to his own collection....(27)

The idea found favor with librarians, and cooperation, on a limited scale, began among libraries in the early part of 1900. Articles, surveys, and reports about interlibrary loans were published, and the issue became important enough to be discussed at the American Library Association annual conference in May 1911 at Pasadena, California, and at the following year's conference in Ottawa.(28) By 1916 "Regulations for the Conduct of Interlibrary Loans" were suggested at the American Library Association conference in Asbury Park, New Jersey, and at the midwinter meeting of the council on 29 December 1916 in Chicago the "Code of Practice for Interlibrary Loans" was presented and later approved in 1917. Its purpose was twofold:

1. To aid research that is calculated to advance the boundaries of knowledge, by the loan of unusual books not readily accessible elsewhere

2. To augment the supply of the average book to the average reader (the graduate student who has a thesis to prepare stands midway between these two extremes)(29)

The 1917 code was revised in 1940 to take into account, among other things, technological developments in photocopying by including the rule that a library, when applying for a loan, should state whether a photocopy would suffice as a substitute. Few libraries charged the user for interlibrary service aside from postage fees. The revision also stated that "libraries were to observe the provision of Copyright Law and the right of literary property in making reproductions."(30) The 1940 code was

replaced in 1952 and then revised in 1956 to incor-
porate changes in the appendixes only.   In June 1967,
the Reference Services Division of the American Library
Association adopted the National Interlibrary Loan Code,
which presently governs the lending relations among libraries on the national level.   The code suggests in
its introduction that interlibrary loan requests should be
restricted to materials which cannot be obtained at
moderate cost by other means.   The cost involved in
lending and the conflict in demand necessitated this
restriction.(31)   The code makes it clear that the
borrowing library assumes all charges involved in trans-
portation, insurance, and copying if the lending library finds the charges more than nominal (that is,
postal charges are recommended to be nominal).

It was clear that libraries should join together
and cooperate more closely in order to face the
tremendous increase in publication and to serve their
users efficiently.   In 1967 the Association of Public,
State, School, and College and Research Libraries of
the American Library Association approved a joint
statement on cooperation.   The statement stressed the
need for such cooperation as would satisfy users' needs
and listed the following prerequisites for effective cooperation:(32)

1. Primary responsibility for each type of library
    to its clientele must be defined before inter-
    library cooperation can be established to aug-
    ment service.

2. Effective cooperation depends upon adequate
    resources, administrative capability, and effi-
    cient communications.

3. Although the primary responsibility of each
    library must be respected, each library must

realize its responsibility to the network and assume its appropriate share of responsibility.

4. All libraries must maintain an attitude of flexibility and experimentation.

This concern for resource and service sharing was reflected in federal and state library legislation during the 1960s.

Besides the loss of identity as a problem in resource sharing, libraries face a copyright problem. The Interlibrary Loan Code indicates that the lending library has to decide whether to provide the borrowing library with the original work requested or a photocopy of it. The reproduction of material in this respect is based on the concept of fair use, which reflects, as claimed, the very purpose for which statutory copyright is granted. Libraries in general, and research libraries in particular, have fully developed photocopying services. Being aware of the implications of copyright infringement, with such a high volume of copying, libraries have sought to protect themselves in three ways:

1. They consistently ask their users to observe the doctrine of fair use. This is considered a manifestation of the libraries' good intentions.

2. All libraries require that any photoreproduction be requested in a written statement signed by the patron. This is assumed to serve as a disclaimer on their behalf, since the patron will presumably assume all responsibility for any infringement. There is some doubt, however, regarding the legal validity of such disclaimers.(33)

3. All libraries believe and contend that they are not selling photocopies, but, by analogy on the

basis that "if a library patron buys or borrows paper and a pen from the library and therewith proceeds to commit infringement, can the library be held responsible?"(34)

Interlibrary loans may be refused or neglected so that an agreement to share resources becomes essential. Such agreements have resulted in what are now called networks. Networks are classified by System Development Corporation into four general types:(35)

1. Large network: concerned primarily with large-scale computerized operations (for example, Ohio College Library Center, OCLC)

2. Small network: concerned primarily with user services on a daily basis (for example, Tri-State College Library Cooperation, TCLC in Pennsylvania, Ohio, and West Virginia)

3. Limited purpose network cooperating in limited special subject area (for example, The Consortium of Western Colleges and Universities in California)

4. Limited purpose network cooperating in reference or interlibrary loans (for example, Delaware Rapid Interlibrary Loan, DRILL)

Among the well-known networks in the United States and abroad is the Interlibrary Loan Service of the National Library of Medicine (NLM), better known as the Medical Literature Analysis and Retrieval System (MEDLARS).
    Under Section 72 (Functions of the Library) of Public Law 941 (84th Congress), the National Library of Medicine Act, which was signed in August 1956, the following legal base for the library is provided:

> Section 372 (a) The Surgeon General, through the
> Library ... shall ... make available, through loans,
> photographic or other copying procedures or other-
> wise, such materials in the library as he deems
> appropraite....

In 1957, NLM initiated a new loan policy which included
the following functions:(36)

1. Individuals are permitted to use the collection on
    the premises on a noncirculating basis. National
    Library of Medicine lends material only to other
    libraries. The library operation became an "inter-
    library loan service."

2. As a rule, all material in the library is available
    for loan; however, ordinary current publications
    that are considered available in any library are
    not subject to loans.

3. National Library of Medicine has the right to
    determine whether the loan will be made in
    original or in photocopy form. The determina-
    tion is based on many factors (for example,
    copyright restrictions, valuableness, and physical
    condition).

4. Photocopies used as a substitute to borrowing
    libraries are to be supplied free of charge.
    These copies can also be retained by those
    libraries.

In 1963, less than ten years after the policy was initiated, requests for interlibrary loans to NLM totaled
158,000, an increase of 22.5 percent, over the previous
year. Of these requests 128,000 were filled by photocopies and 6,500 were filled by loan of original
materials. A review of the statistics of this period

indicates that requests for photocopies alone were filled at a rate of one per minute of every working day throughout the year. It has also been estimated that 2,000 libraries abroad received approximately 2,300,000 pages of photocopies.(37)

In January 1964, MEDLARS went into operation to meet the demands of quick retrieval of citations from the rapidly expanding biomedical literature. Some of its main objectives are as follows:

1. To increase the number of journals indexed in *Index Medicus* and reduce the time required for preparing its monthly editions

2. To reduce the duplication of literature by screening activities done by other research libraries in the United States

MEDLARS has three major subdivisions: (a) an input system with skilled indexers working in it, (b) a retrieval system staffed with literature searchers, and (c) a publication system that converts retrieval information into photopositive film. A graphic-image storage and retrieval system has been implemented to permit rapid photocopy retrieval of the full text documents in the library's collection.(38)

There is ample evidence in statistical reports of the success of the NLM network system. As a result, publishers in the medical field voice their objections to the mass production of photocopying and claim that it affects their existence because of subscription freeze. Strangely enough, some medical librarians expressed concern over the same system, but for different reasons. Brandon, for example, recognized the comprehensiveness of the NLM collection which consists of single original copies but noted at the same time, "It seems ludicrous that medical libraries of every size in every part of the nation should think of borrowing my journal directly from the National Library of Medicine instead of seeking it first within their own areas." He concluded, "....Let us use the services of our National Library of Medicine correctly and in perspective...."(39) Sooner or later such wholesale copying was bound to be challenged as copyright infringement.

NOTES

1. *Survey of Copyrighted Material Reproduction Practices in Scientific and Technical Fields.* Chicago: George Fry & Associates, 1962, p. V-I.

2. *Ibid.*

3. *Ibid.*

4. *Dellar* v. *Samuel Goldwyn Inc.,* 104 and F. 2nd 661 (2nd Cir. 1939).

5. W. L. Pforzheimer, "Historical Prospective on Copyright Law and Fair Use." In *Reprography and Copyright Law,* edited by L. Hattery and G. Bush, Washington, D. C.: American Institute of Biological Sciences, 1964.

6. *Folsom* v. *Marsh,* 9 Fed. Cas. 4.901, 2 Story 100 (D. Mass. 1841).

7. Charles F. Gosnell, "The Viewpoint of the Librarian and Library User." In *Copyright Current Viewpoints on History, Laws, Legislation.* edited by A. Kent and H. Lancour. New York: Bowker, 1972, p. 61.

8. Alan Latman, "Fair Use of Copyrighted Works." Study 14, March 1958, Committee on the Judiciary, U.S. Senate, 1960. U.S. Congress, 86th, 2nd Session, "Copyright Law Revision." Study 14, prepared for the Subcommittee on Patent, Tradeworks and Copyrights, Committee on the Judiciary, U.S. Senate. Washington, D.C.: U.S. Government Printing Office, 1960. Committee Print.

9. *Ibid.*

10. Ralph Shaw, *Literary Property in the United States.*
    Metuchen, N. J.: Scarecrow Press, 1950.

11. ——"Publication and Distribution of Scientific Literature."
    College and Research Library 17: 294-301 (July,
    1956).

12. ——*Literary Property in the United States*, p. 99.

13. Miles O. Price, "Photocopying by Libraries and Copyright:
    A Precis." *Library Trends* 8: 438 (Jan. 1960).

14. J. S. Saunders, "Origin of the Gentleman's Agreement of
    1935." In *Reprography and Copyright Law,* edited by
    L. Hattery and G. Bush, p. 160. Washington, D. C.:
    American Institute of Biological Sciences, 1964.

15. R. D. Brinkley, *Manual on Methods of Reproducing Research
    Materials.* Ann Arbor, Mich.: Edwards Brothers, Inc.,
    1936, p. IV.

16. Saunders, *op. cit.,* p. 164.

17. F. Melcher, Memorandum in Saunders, *op. cit.,* p. 165.

18. "Fair Use in Photocopying: Report on Single Copies."
    ALA Bulletin 55: 572 (June 1961).

19. *Association of Research Libraries News Letter*, No. 53,
    p. 4 (March 3, 1972).

20. Becker, Joseph, ed., *Proceedings of the Conference on
    Interlibrary Communications and Information Networks,
    Airlie House, Sept. 28-Oct. 2, 1970.* Chicago:
    American Library Association, 1971.

21. V. W. Clapp, *The Future of the Research Library.*
    Urbana, Ill.¾ University of Illinois Press, 1964.

22. R. E. Chapin, "Limits of Local Self-Sufficiency." *Proceedings
    of the Conference on Interlibrary Communications and
    Information Networks,* edited by Joseph Becker, p. 54.
    Chicago: American Library Association, 1971.

23. American Library Association, *Interlibrary Cooperation.*

Chicago: American Library Association, 1967.

24. Chapin, *op. cit.,* p. 58.

25. Ralph Blasingame, "The Great Library in Sky Prototype."
    Library Journal 97: 1771 (May 15, 1972).

26. D. J. Desola Price, *Science Since Babylon.* New Haven:
    Yale University Press, 1961.

27. S. S. Green, "The Lending of Books to one Another by
    Librarians." *Library Journal* 1: 15-16 (Sept. 1876).

28. "Papers and Proceedings of the Ottawa Conference,
    June 26-July 2, 1912." *ALA Bulletin* 6: 57-353
    (1912).

29. Mary Stephanie, "A History of the Interlibrary Loan Code."
    Wisconsin Library Bulletin. 57: 274 (Sep.-Oct. 1961).

30. *Ibid.,* p. 275.

31. S. K. Thomason. *Interlibrary Loan Procedure Manual.*
    Chicago: American Library Association, 1970, p. 1.

32. American Library Association, *op. cit.*

33. Charles F. Gosnell, "Copyright." In *Copying Methods Manual,*
    edited by W. R. Hawken, p. 314. Chicago:
    American Library Association, 1966.

34. *Ibid.*

35. John J. Fetterman, "Resource Sharing in Libraries– Why?"
    In *Resource Sharing in Libraries,* edited by Allen
    Kent, p. 9. New York: Marcel Dekker, 1974.

36. F. B. Rogers, "The Loan Policy of the National Library
    of Medicine." *Bulletin of the Medical Library
    Association* 45: 486-493 (Oct. 1957).

37. J. H. Roe and T. R. Cassidy, "The Interlibrary Loan
    Service of the National Library of Medicine." *College
    and Research Libraries* 26: 47-48 (Jan. 1965)

38. L. Karel; C. Austin; M. Cummings, "Computerized

Bibliographic Services for Biomedicine." *Science* 148: 771-771 (May 1965).

39. A. N. Brandon, "A National Problem." *Bulletin of the Medical Library Association* 52: 442 (April 1964).

Chapter 3

THE UNITED STATES COPYRIGHT LAW

In 1785 Lord Mansfield said:

> [We] must take care to guard against two extremes, equally prejudicial: the one, that men of ability, who have employed their time for the service of the community, may not be deprived of their just merit, and the reward to their ingenuity and labour; the other, that the world may not be deprived of improvements, nor the progress of the arts be retarded.(1)

In an attempt to reconcile these extremes, copyright laws have been developed. Macaulay's illustrative statement that "copyright is a tax on readers for the purpose of giving a bounty to the writers"(2) also gives a true picture of the conflict of interest between the copyright owner and the user of his work. The fact was, and still is, that the right of those who write and publish and the interest of those who use what is written and published come into conflict and "it has been a state of continuing discontent."

The raison d'etre of copyright is related to the quality of the culture of any nation, which can be judged only by its intellectual and artistic works. Such productivity appears to be strongly influenced by the encouragement and protection granted to the creators of cultural works. This public interest did not escape the eyes of our founding fathers, who set forth the following

provision respecting copyright in the U.S. Constitution,
Article 1, Section 8:

> The Congress shall have Power ... To promote the
> Progress of Science and useful Arts, by securing
> for limited time to Authors and Inventors the
> exclusive Right to their respective Writings and
> Discoveries.

In essence, the copyright is the right of an author
(or the publisher who takes an exclusive license from
the author) to control the reproduction of his intellectual
creation.   This is conceivable only if he discloses his
work to others and makes it possible for them to reproduce it.   The protection of copyright can be applied
only after the work has been disclosed.   As long as the
author keeps his work in his own possession, the creator's exclusive control is physical rather than legal.   If
an author chooses not to release his work for publication, then his right is derived from the common law.
This right is permanent as long as the work stays un-
disclosed.   When the work is published it can be protected only for a limited time by statutory copyright,
and all rights under the common law copyright cease to
exist.
   The author's common law right is based on the
principle of natural justice.   An author's writing is
considered a "product of intellectual labor and as much
his own property as the substance on which he wrote
it."   An analogy lies in the Irish King Diarmed's
statement, in settling the property rights in a manuscript, "To every cow its calf."(3)
   Copyright is considered a form of unique property.
Because it is intangible, the copyright is incapable of
being possessed except when it is embodied in a tangi-
ble object (for example, a book, journal, tape, or film).

Justice Holmes defined the property right in copyright as follows:

> The notion of property starts, I suppose, from confirmed possession of a tangible object and consists in the right to exclude others from interference with the more or less free doing with it as one wills. But in copyright, property has reached a more abstract expression. The right to exclude is not directed to an object in possession or owned, but is now in vacuo, so to speak. It restrains the spontaneity of men where, but for it, there would be nothing of any kind to hinder their doing as they saw fit. It is a prohibition of conduct remote from the persons or tangibles of the party having the right. It may be infringed a thousand miles from the owner and without his ever becoming aware of the wrong.(4)

Some theoreticians, particularly in the Napoleonic school of thought, consider copyright a personal right of the author, and some consider it a combination of personal and property rights. An author's creation usually reflects his personality and, in many instances, can be identified with him. The only weakness in this school of thought, however, is that the author's right continues to exist after his death and can be assigned to others. Both are unknown characteristics of personal rights. The countries that follow the theory of personal right (for example, France) have included in their copyright law certain provisions for the author's "moral right," to protect misrepresentation or injuries to his personal reputation. Some of the rights granted to the author are the following:

1. His right to have his name appear on all copies of his work.

2. His right to prevent the attribution of his work to someone else and vice versa

3. His right to ascertain that any reproduction of his
work is free of distortion.

The author in these countries can waive any of these
rights in certain cases, but not if these moral rights are
assignable.   The United States does not subscribe to the
personal right theory.   Assignability of the copyright has
always been a fundamental feature of the law in the
United States.   This was reiterated by the register of
copyrights when he stated that one of the purposes of
the statutory law is to give authors their due reward in
return for their contributions to society.(5)   The question
is, What is the reward due to the author and how big
is it?

Not everyone sees the provision of law in the same
light.   Copyright has different meanings for different
persons.   To the author it is a recognition and a way
of earning his livelihood.   To the publisher it is the
exclusive right of production and dissemination needed
for the financial support of his business.   To the
reader it is a part of the price he pays to have information that he wants.   To the researcher it is a
necessary reward to an author that may create a potential obstacle in the way of his own work.(6)

The constitutional provision empowers Congress to
decide what the exclusive rights of the author are in
light of the primary purpose of promoting science and
useful arts.   Copyright does not preclude others from
using the ideas presented by the author of a published
work.   Copyright protection pertains only to the form
in which the author expresses his ideas.   Anyone,
therefore, is free to create his own expression of the
same idea as long as he does not copy the author's
form of expression.   The dividing line, however, is not
always sharply defined.

As previously stated, Congress has enacted and revised several times three copyright acts since 1790. The most comprehensive is the Copyright Act of 4 March 1909, amended in 1912 to include motion pictures. This act was codified in 1947 as Title 17 of the U.S. Code and, except for minor amendments, is our present copyright law.

Since the control granted the author over his work is absolute, many consider copyright a monopoly. And since the control is rather unlimited, it could become an undue restraint on the dissemination of the work. On the other hand, copyright prevents reproduction of the same work, which in turn encourages independent creation to compete with it in the market place. The only possible monopoly is when many works are pooled together and controlled by one person or one company.

The first section of the statute lists the exclusive rights of the copyright owner. These include, among others, his right "to print, reprint, publish, copy and vend the copyrighted work."

This protection also extends to "all the copyable component parts" (Title 17, U.S. Code, Section 3). An article, therefore, is a "component part" of the periodical in which it appears.(7) It should be noted, however, that this is the case only if the author gives an exclusive license to the publisher; otherwise, the author's copyright notice must appear on the article.

The *Oxford English Dictionary* provides several definitions for the word "copy" ("to imitate;" "without reference to an original;" and so forth). It also defines "copy" as "plenty, abundance (copious quantity)."(8) The same dictionary makes it clear that during the Middle Ages there was an aura of deceit associated with the word "copy." From the late 16th century until Victorian times "copy" and "counterfeit" were almost synonymous. It was also a favorite

Victorian habit to call a person a "pale copy" of another.

On the other hand, *Black's Law Dictionary* defines copy as "a transcript or a double of an original writing."(9)   And, as it relates to the law of copyright, a copy is "a reproduction or duplication of a thing or that which comes so near to the original as to give to every person seeing it the idea created by the original."(10)

An unchallenged but popular thesis is that the verb "copy" as used in Section 1 (a) of the copyright law was intended to refer to the making of multiple copies and not to the making of single copies.   The same intention is attributed to the verb "print" in the same section.   Both verbs relate to the production of multicopies which makes it possible to publish and market a work, "an entity of which an essential characteristic is plurality."(11)   Furthermore, there is nothing in the legislative history of the copyright law to suggest that its meaning has changed or been extended to include single copying.   In consequence, it is incorrect to assume that the verbs "copy" and "print," as referred to in Title 17 of the U.S. Code, apply to the making of single copies.   In fact, the late publisher Richard Rogers Bowker defined the right to copy as "... this work ... covers the duplicating or multiplying of copies within the stated scope of the [1909] statute."(12)

Although the author's rights are exclusive and monopolistic, his interests, on the other hand, coincide with those of the public, as both will benefit from the author's work.   However, in case of conflict, the interest of the author must yield to the public welfare.   Accordingly, the U.S. copyright law has imposed certain limitations and conditions on copyright protection:

1. The rights of the copyright owner do not extend to certain uses of the work (for example, performance of literary work in churches for religious purposes).

2. The term of copyright is limited as required by the Constitution (the time is 28 years renewable to another 28 years).

3. A copyright notice is required in published works. The published material for which the author does not wish to obtain a copyright is therefore left free of restrictions.

4. The registration of copyright and the transfer of ownership are required. This facilitates the means of determining the status and ownership of copyright claims.

These limitations and conditions may be essential in the public interest, but they are not so burdensome or strict as to deprive the author from securing copyright or from collecting his just reward.

In general, copyright protection can be secured for all kinds of creative works (literary, artistic, musical, and so forth). However, the U.S. Copyright Code, Title 17, Section 5, lists the following classes of works that can be copyrighted:

Books, including composite and cyclopedic works, dictionaries, gazettes, and other compilations

Periodicals, including newspapers

Lectures, sermons, addresses (prepared for oral delivery)

Dramatic or dramatic-musical compositions

Musical compositions

Maps

Works of art; models or designs for works of art

Reproductions of a work of art

Drawings for plastic works of scientific or technical
character

Photographs

Prints or pictorial illusions, including prints or
labels used for articles or merchandise

Motion-picture photoplays

Motion-pictures other than photoplays

Sound recordings *

The copyright Revision bill, pending in the U.S.
Senate, covers all the above-mentioned works under
seven more generic categories as follows:

1. Literary works

2. Musical works, including any accompanying works

3. Dramatic works, including any accompanying
music

4. Pantomines and choreographic work

5. Pictorial, graphic, and sculptural works

6. Motion pictures and other audio-visual works

7. Sound recordings

*Section 5(n) was added by an act of 15 October 1971,
Public Law 92-140, 85 Stat. 391.

Under our present copyright law (Sections 10, 11, 13, 19, 20, and 21), an author or a publisher who has obtained an exclusive license from an author can secure copyright by publishing copies of his work bearing a copyright notice. The notice consists of the word "copyright" or any of the two accepted abbreviations (Corp. or   in addition to the name of the copyright owner and the year of the first publication. Therefore, if a published work lacks the copyright notice, one has to assume that it is in the public domain and not protected by the statute, and vice versa. Some works, however, may consist of both types (for example, a copyrighted new introduction to an old book in the public domain). In this case the copyright notice protects the introduction only and not the rest of the publication whether the notice is on the title page of the whole work or whether it indicates that specifically or not.

The United States, like most other countries, requires two copies of the best printing of every work published to be deposited promptly (Section 407 of the bill requires a deposit within three months) in the Copyright Office with the application and the required fees for the registration of copyright. The deposited copies are used to build the collection in the Library of Congress and for exchange with domestic and foreign libraries.

Goldman defines a work in the public domain as a work which is "free of any copyright restrictions [and] is available for reproduction or any other use by everyone. Once in the public domain a work cannot thereafter be made subject to copyright."(13)

A work falls in the public domain for three Reasons: (a) the work is published without the copyright

notice; (b) the work is a government publication; or
(c) the copyright on the work expires.

A.   Works Published Without Copyright Notice

It is interesting to note that the United States is
the only country that requires a copyright notice.   The
new revision bill continues to ask for the same requirement because of its convenience as a source of information regarding the status of the work and the date of
its publication.   The bill, however, proposes a less con-
stricting requirement of the notice.   The copyright owner,
under the proposed bill, can register his copyright claim
regardless of the absence of the notice.   In any case,
an author cannot sue a user for liability if the latter
infringed innocently due to the lack of such notice.
(See Section 21 in the present law and Section 405
in the revision bill.)   The new bill, however, would
permit a court to allow recovery if the infringer
profited from the infringement.   The bill also estab-
lishes a five-year time limit, after which the work goes
into the public domain if there has been no effort to
correct the error or register the claim.

B.   United States Government Publications

If the work is a government publication, Section 8
of the copyright statute is very specific in stating, "Copyright Not to Subsist in ... Government Publications."
However, the publication or re-publication by the government of any copyrighted material should not be construed as an abridgement or an annulment of the copyright.   The revision bill follows the same rule but does
not preclude the U.S. government from receiving and
holding copyrights transferred to it by assignment, be-
quest, or otherwise.   (See Section 105 of the revision

bill S.1361.) On the state and local government level, nonlegal documents are copyrightable.

In trying to define a publication of the United States Government two questions are asked:

1. Is it a work produced for the government by one or more of its employees, whether it is published by the government or otherwise.

2. Is it a work published by the government and produced by anyone regardless of his employment?

Since the present copyright statute did not define the term, the case law and the Copyright Law Office consider "government publication" as

> a work produced for the Government by its employees ... [and] that any work so produced is not copyrightable, even though it is issued by a private publisher; and that any work privately produced may be copyrighted even though the author permits the Government to publish it.(14)

Recently, there was a strong debate concerning the use and copying of government-supported research reports and publications by librarians and scholars. The argument, based on the fact that the reason and justification of the copyright provision is the public benefit, was stated in the House of Representatives report accompanying the 1909 copyright bill:

> The Constitution does not establish copyright, but provides that Congress shall have the power to grant such rights if it thinks best. Not primarily for the benefit of the author, but primarily for the benefit of the public, such rights are given.(15)

Along the same line, the Committee on Scientific and technical Communications of the National Academy of Sciences and the National Academy of Engineering stated in a 1969 report on scientific and technical communications:

> In the matter of copyrighting publications resulting from government sponsored work, a policy which abrogates the protection of copyright under these conditions could be based on the principle that information developed at the taxpayers expense should be available for anyone to publish or disseminate as he may see fit.(16)

Many librarians and scholars suggest a "royalty-free use which should be extended to all users of publications derived from Government sponsored funding."(17) In addition, they believe that the author in such situations has been reimbursed for his time through a grant or government salary and is more concerned with having his report published than with securing a copyright protection. Authors, especially of scientific and technical works, derive prestige and benefit from the reactions they receive from their colleagues and have no expectation of receiving royalties. Consequently, some federal agencies, in the late 1960s and early 1970s, adopted policies to protect their right to copy, royalty-free, works resulting from awards granted by them. For example, the Public Health Service policy reads in part as follows:

> Except as may otherwise be provided under the terms and conditions of the award, the grantee may copyright without prior approval any publications, films, or similar materials developed or resulting from research projects supported by a grant under this part, subject, however, to a royalty-free nonexclusive license or right be the Government to reproduce, translate, publish, use,

> disseminate, and dispose of such materials and
> authorize others to do so.(18)

Recipients of government grants stress the value of copyright as an incentive for their creations. Publishers support this view and argue that their participation in the dissemination of research and ideas sponsored by the government should not affect the fact that they have to maintain a financial balance in their businesses and that copyright protects their interest and existence.

C. Expiration of Copyright

If the copyright on the work expires, Section 24 of the present law provides the following:

> The copyright secured by this title shall endure for twenty-eight years from the date of first publication, ... the proprietor of such copyright shall be entitled to a renewal and extension of the copyright in such work for further term of twenty-eight years when application for such renewal and extension shall have been made to the Copyright Office and duly registered therein within one year prior to the expiration of the original term of copyright ... and that the widow, widower, or children of the author, if the author be not living, or if such author's widow, widower, or children be not living, then the author's executor, or in the absence of a will, his next of kin shall be entitled to a renewal and extension of the copyright in such work for a further term of twenty-eight years.

Macaulay, inspired by the constitutional provision, warned in one of his speeches that copyright protection "ought not to last a day longer than is necessary."(19) The period of protection has nevertheless increased gradually in the past two centuries from two years to the present 56 years of the initial and renewal terms.

At the beginning of the 20th century a new approach advocated, as a complete term for copyright protection, the life of the author plus 50 years, which is similar to the terms provided for in most other countries. The renewal requirement, however, was retained in the 1909 act. This was decided upon by Congress in an attempt to protect the author, who is usually in a disadvantageous bargaining position at the initial stage of getting his work published. Once the true value of the work is known, the author or his heir can negotiate a better contract for the renewal of copyright. The retention of the renewal requirement was also a way of permitting the bulk of copyrighted material to fall in the public domain after 28 years, since approximately 28 percent of the publications eligible for renewal are not renewed.(20)

On the other hand, some considered the 56-year period too short because the bulk of copyrighted material falls in the public domain usually during a time in the life of the aging creator when he really needs to collect royalties. This criticism gained more support particularly since the life expectancy for an average person increased by 20 years since 1909.

Section 302 (a) of the new revision bill, however, changed the present term of copyright for the first time by eliminating the renewal provisions and proposing a copyright term that lasts for the life of the author, plus 50 years. This was calculated to equal approximately 75 years of protection, which was not viewed as excessive in light of the increase in life expectancy. This approach was also proposed as a desirable move to make the U.S. law consistent with the general international practice.(21)

Under the proposed bill, Section 302 (b), work prepared by two or more authors who did not work for hire could be protected for the life of the last surviving author and 50 years after *his* death.

The new duration of copyright as proposed by S.1361 could create a hardship for the librarian and the scholar if the work has anonymous, pseudonymous, or corporate authorships since the life of the author can be ascertained only if he is known. To cope with such situations, Section 302 (c) of the bill proposed a copyright term of 75 years from the year of the first publication of the work of 100 years from the year of its creation, whichever expires first. However, if the identity of the author is discovered, then the life-plus-50-years rule applies.

However, works identified by authors do not necessarily eliminate the user's or the librarian's hardship in ascertaining the date of death, particularly if the author is less known. Consequently, the proposed bill required the register of copyrights to maintain a correct record of the death of authors of copyrighted works. (See Section 302 (d) S.1361.)

The new bill proposed some significant changes, and among those that relate to libraries and information centers are the following three important propositions:

1. The proposed changes in the duration of copyright constitute, for the first time, a departure from the traditional common law copyright protection which the United States inherited from the colonial period. Since the pending revision bill proposed a maximum term of protection of 75 to 100 years from the date of creation, the permanent common law copyright on unpublished works would cease to exist.

2. The Fair Use Doctrine, which has been developed by the courts over many years, is defined simply as the "safety valve" or the

> doctrine ... [that] permits the reproduction, for
> legitimate purposes, or material taken from a
> copyrighted work to a limited extent that will
> not cut into the copyright owner's potential
> market for the sale of copies.(22)

In its application, the courts were left free to determine whether a given situation involves fair use or otherwise. This freedom in consideration and application gave the courts the opportunity to adapt the doctrine to the changing situation in individual cases. The omission of the doctrine from the 1909 act was therefore purposeful. During the past 60 years inclusion of the doctrine was attempted in almost every proposed revision of the copyright law but none materialized. The new revision bill S.1361, however, proposed the inclusion of the doctrine of fair use in Section 107:

> Notwithstanding the provisions of Section 106 [on the
> exclusive rights in copyrighted works], the fair use
> of a copyrighted work, including such use by repro-
> duction in copies or phonorecords or by any other
> means specified by that Section, for purposes such as
> criticism, comment, news reporting, teaching, scholarship,
> or research, is not an infringement of copyright. In
> determining whether the use made of a work in any
> particular case is a fair use the factors to be con-
> sidered include:
> 1. the purpose and character of the use;
> 2. the nature of the copyrighted work;
> 3. the amount and substantiality of the portion
>   used in relation to the copyrighted work as
>   a whole; and
> 4. the effect of the use upon the potential market
>   for the value of the copyrighted work.

This will be the first time that the doctrine has gained statutory recognition that fair use of copyrighted works is not infringement. Furthermore,

the six activities cited in the proposed section
are cited only as examples and are not to be
construed as exclusive.(23)   Copyright owners
(that is, authors and publishers), however, are not
in favor of Section 107 on the grounds that
having statutory fair use will encourage and in-
duce more infringement on copyrights and that
the listing of the six permissible activities
"would imply that anything remotely connected
with those purposes would constitute fair use."
(24)   Librarians and educators, on the other
hand, are not happy with the middle of the
road approach of the provision.   The language
of the section, as they claim, is vague and does
not specify clearly what is considered fair or unfair use of copyrighted materials.   Much debate
about this vital and controversial matter is still
in progress.

3. Another first is the statutory recognition of the
   conflict between the public right and the pro-
   prietory interest evident in the inclusion of library photocopying in Section 108 of the proposed bill.

In 1961 the register of copyrights recognized, in his
report on the general revision of the copyright law, that
photocopying by libraries was becoming an important
issue "which merits special consideration."(25)   In his
preliminary draft of a copyright bill, the register included a provision permitting specialized research libraries
to provide users with a copy of one article or a part
of any copyrighted material without investigation or prior
permission.   Copies of an entire work were also permitted, if the work was out of print, providing that
the library warned the user, in writing, that the work
was copyrighted.   Both librarians and publishers were in

opposition to such inclusion. Both indicated that they would rather rely on the Fair Use Doctrine than a statutory permission like that in question. With this strong opposition, the revision bill (H.R.2512) passed the House of Representatives in 1967 without any provisions dealing with library photocopying per se. However, when the bill (known as S.1361) moved to the Senate, the American Library Association and the Association of Research Libraries, plus many other library associations, proposed a provision allowing libraries to make single copies for their users. This was discussed by the author-publisher group, and finally the Senate Judiciary Subcommittee, in an attempt to reconcile the different interests involved, introduced Section 108 to Senate on 10 December 1969. The proposed provision reads as follows (Section 8):

> 108. Limitations on exclusive rights: Reproduction by libraries and archives
>
> a. Notwithstanding the provisions of Section 106, it is not an infringement of copyright for a library or archives, or any of its employees acting within the scope of their employment, to reproduce no more than one copy or phonorecord of a work, or distribute such copy or phonorecord, under the conditions specified by this Section and if
>
> > 1. The reproduction or distribution is made without any purpose of direct or indirect commercial advantage; and
> >
> > 2. The collections of the library or archives are open (i) open to the public, or (ii) available not only to researchers affiliated with the library or archives or with the institution of which it is a part, but also to other persons doing research in a specialized field.
>
> b. The rights of reproduction and distribution under this Section apply to a copy or phonorecord of an unpublished work duplicated in facsimile form solely for purposes of preservation and security or

for deposit for research use in another library or archives of the type described by clause (2) of subsection (a), if the copy or phonorecord reproduced is currently in the collections of the library or archives.

c. The right of reproduction under this section applies to a copy or phonorecord of a published work duplicated in facsimile form solely for the purpose of replacement of a copy or phonorecord that is damaged, deteriorating, lost, or stolen, if the library or archives has, after a reasonable effort, determined that an unused replacement cannot be obtained at a normal price from commonly-known trade sources in the United States, including authorized reproducing services.

d. The rights of reproduction and distribution under this section apply to a copy of a work, other than a musical work, a pictorial, graphic or sculptural work, or a motion picture or other audio-visual work, made at the request of a user of the collections of the library or archives, including a user who makes his request through another library or archives, if:

1. The user has established to the satisfaction of the library or archives that an unused copy cannot be obtained at a normal price from commonly known trade sources in the United States, including authorized reproducing services;

2. The copy becomes the property of the user, and the library, or archives has had no notice that the copy would be used for any purpose other than private study, scholarship, or research; and

3. The library or archives displays prominently, at the place where orders are accepted, and includes on its order form, a warning of copyright in accordance with requirements that the Register of Copyrights shall prescribe by regulation.

e. Nothing in this section—

1. shall be construed to impose liability for copyright infringement upon a library or archives or its employees for the unsupervised use of reproducing equipment located on its

premises, provided that such equipment displays a notice that the making of a copy may be subject to the copyright law;

2. excuses a person who uses such reproducing equipment or who requests a copy under subsection (d) from liability for copyright infringement for any such act, or for any use of such;

3. in any way affects the right of fair use as provided in Section 107, or any contractual obligations assumed by the library or archives when it obtained a copy or phonorecord of the work for its collections.

f. The rights of reproducing or distributing "no more than one copy or phonorecord" in accordance with this section extend to the related and unrelated reproduction or distribution of a single copy or phonorecord of the same work on separate occasions, but do not extend to cases where the library or archives, or its employee, is aware or has substantial reason to believe that it is engaging in the related or concerted reproduction or distribution of multiple copies or phonorecords of the same work, whether on one occasion or over a period of time, and whether intended for aggregate use by one individual or for separate use by the individual members of a group.

The first impression one may get from reading Section 108 in general and Section 108 (e) in particular is that the proposed provision reiterates the doctrine of fair use. A close look, however, proves that Section 108, in essence, puts certain limitations and conditions on fair use, a contradictory approach to what the bill tries to accomplish in Section 107, which was drafted nonspecifically. Although it addressed itself to the problem partially, the bill, for the first time, permitted libraries that are open to the public and researchers in a specific field to make one copy (a) for the preservation purpose of unpublished works; (b) for damaged, stolen, or lost copyrighted works; and (c) for a user who has to prove that the requested copy is from a

work that is unavailable from trade sources or authorized reproducing services.

The bill also defined, for the first time, the right
of libraries to reproduce "no more than one copy,"
which would extend to reproducing one copy on a
certain occasion or several "isolated and unrelated"
separate occasions, providing that the library believes
it is not engaging in the reproduction of multiple
copies as such. In this respect the proposed provision
has eliminated specifically, again for the first time, any
liability for infringement upon the library or its employees for the unsupervised use of copying machines located in the library, providing that such machines dis-
play a warning about copyright law.

Librarians, however, were disatisfied with the
language of the bill. First, it imposed restrictions on
its application, which is rather burdensome and unwork-
able (for example, the cost and delay in ascertaining
that a given work is not available through commonly
known trade sources is a hindrance to efficient and
prompt library service). Second, there is no fool-
proof way of checking the user's purpose or motive
for requesting a single copy of a copyrighted work.
Third, the proposed exemptions apply to libraries open
to the public and not to private research libraries (for
example, a library in a research laboratory).

Section 108 is, without a doubt, a controversial
one as it relates to the problem of photocopying by
libraries. The questions involved are as follows:

1. The revision bill made it clear that there is no
   absolute right of libraries to copy. However,
   libraries have no right to deprive the user of
   his lawful right to have access to knowledge.
   Copyright was not intended, at any time, to
   suppress access to information.

2. The concept of accessibility of information is not debatable, but the creation, processing, and availability of information come at a cost and have to be provided for if the flow and availability of information are to continue. The question is, Who will pay for this commodity?

3. The proposed bill may impose no liability for copyright infringement upon the library or its staff, but this is clearly at the expense of the strict and rigorous search of the trade sources and the examination of the user's intentions. Librarians, in complying with the law, may not be considered violators, but must they be, in the meantime, enforcers of the publisher's rights?

4. The bill did not discuss copying practice through interlibrary loans, resource sharing, and cooperative systems and networks. Could a library as a unit in a network make use of the provisions provided for in Section 108? Is making a single copy for a sister library upon request equal to making a single copy for an individual? Is there any difference between system use (which is purposeful and substantial) and individual use (which is sporadic and infrequent)?

5. Is a single copy of a complete article from a journal considered a fair use or an infringement?

The writer believes that the answers, although difficult and undoubtedly debatable, lie in the difference between moral and material objectives and obligations. The difficulty in answering these questions is that both objectives, although contradictory, are combined and form the basis for information as a commodity at both its input and output ends.

Any solution must ensure that information is readily available and that access to it is guaranteed. However, the success and enforcibility of any solution is dependent on the will and the commitment of those involved in the information and communication community.

NOTES

1. *Sayre* v. *Moore,* 1 East 361.102 Eng. Rep. 139.140 (K..B.. 1785).

2. Thomas Babington Macaulay, *Macaulay's Speeches on Copyright and Lincoln's Address at Cooper Union, Together with Abridgment of Parliamentary Debates of 1841 and 1842 on Copyright, and Extracts from Douglas's Columbus Speech.* Edited by Charles Robert Gaston. New York: Ginn and Co., 1941.

3. S. Breyer, "The Uneasy Case for Copyright: A Study of Copyright in Books, Photocopies and Computer Programs." *Harvard Law Review* 84: 285 (Dec. 1970).

4. *White-Smith Music Publishing Co.* v. *Apollo Co.* 209 US 1(1908).

5. *Report of the Register of Copyrights on the General Revision of the U.S. Copyright Law House Committee on the Judiciary.* 87th Congress, 1st Session 5 (Committee Print, 1961).

6. Abe A. Goldman, "The Concept of the Law of Copyright." *Reprography and Copyright Law,* p. 11. Edited by L. Hattery and G. Bush. Rochelle Park, N. J.: Hayden Book Co., 1973.

7. *Inter-City Press, Inc.* v. *Siegfried,* 172 F., Supp. 37 (W.D. Mo. 1958).

8. *Oxford English Dictionary.* Oxford: Clarenden Press, 1933, Vol. 11, pp. 978-979.

9. *Black's Law Dictionary,* 4th ed. St. Paul, Minn.: West,

1951, p. 405.

10. *McConnor* v. *Kaufman,* 49, F Supp., (S.D. N.Y., 1943), pp. 738-744.

11. V. W. Clapp, *Copyright—a Librarian's View.* Washington, D. C.: Association of Research Libraries, 1968, p. 25.

12. R. R. Bowker, *Copyright: Its History and Its Law.* New York: Houghton Mifflin Co., 1912, p. 53.

13. Abe A. Goldman, "Copyright as It Affects Libraries: Legal Implications." In *Copyright Current Viewpoints on History, Laws, Legislation.* edited by A. Kent and H. Lancour. New York: Bowker, 1972, p. 36.

14. Charles F. Gosnell, "The Copying Grab Bag: Observation on the New Copyright Legislation." *ALA Bulletin* 60: 32 (Jan. 1966).

15. U.S. Congress, 2nd Session, Feb. 22, 1909, accompanying H.R. 28192. "A Bill to Amend and Consolidate the Acts Respecting Copyright," p. 6.

16. Committee on Scientific and Technical Communication of the National Academy of Engineering, *Scientific and Technical Communication: A Pressing National Problem and Recommendations for Its Solution.* Washington, D. C.: National Academy of Science, [1969], p. 232-233.

17. Johanna Elenore Tallman, "Opinion Paper: An Affirmative Statement on Copyright Debate." *Journal of the American Society for Information Science* 25: 146 (May-June 1974).

18. Code of Federal Regulation, Title 42—Public Health, p. 118.

19. Macaulay, *op. cit.,* p. 23.

20. Cambridge Research Institute, *Omnibus Copyright Revision: Cooperative Analysis of the Issues.* Washington, D. C.: American Society for Information Science, 1973, p. 124.

21. Hearings on H.R. 4347, before Subcommittee no. 3 of the House Committee on the Judiciary, 89th Congress, 1st Session [1965], p. 1867.

22. Goldman, *op. cit.*, p. 39.

23. H.R. REP. no. 83, 90th Congress, 1st Session (1967), p. 29.

24. Cambridge Research Institute, *op. cit.*, p. 38.

25. U.S. Copyright Office, *Copyright Law Revision Studies Prepared for the Subcommittee on Patents, Trademarks and Copyrights of the Committee on the Judiciary United States Senate,* Study 15, 86th Congress, 2nd Session (Committee Print, 1960).

Chapter 4

THE WILLIAMS & WILKINS COMPANY v.
THE UNITED STATES

On 1 May, 1967, Dr. Martin Cummings, director
of the National Library of Medicine (NLM), received
a letter from Mr. William M. Passano, chairman of
the board of the Williams & Wilkins Company (W & W),
a publisher of medical journals in Baltimore, Maryland.
The letter said, in part:

> Since NLM may, from time to time, be requested
> to make copies of articles from journals published by
> the Williams and Wilkins Company, it seems desirable
> that I explain to you our policy in this matter. We
> are glad to give our permission for the copying of
> articles which appear in our journals provided the per-
> son making the copies pays us a royalty of 2¢ per
> page per copy for the privilege of copying the
> material on which we hold the copyright.
>
> In the absence of a royalty payment, no one has our
> permission to copy this material and any copying which
> should take place we would consider to be an infringe-
> ment of our copyright....(1)

This marked the beginning of the eight-year saga of
the *Williams & Wilkins Company* v. *the United States*
which ended in February 1975 in the Supreme Court.

In reaction, Cummings ordered the library staff to
stop photocopying all W & W journals until further
notice. He also referred and discussed the matter with
the general council of the Department of Health, Education and Welfare, the parent agency of NLM. On the

advice of the general council, Cummings informed Passano that NLM photocopying was within the judicial doctrine of fair use and that photocopying of W & W journals would be resumed.

In the meantime, Passano wrote to F. J. L. Blasingame, executive vice-president of the American Medical Association (AMA), requesting that the AMA refrain from photocopying W & W journals without paying royalties. He also wrote:

> Otherwise, you and we and the country can look for-
> ward to a bitter future of complete government sub-
> sidy and control of your and our scientific press....
> While I realize there will be an increase in our
> clerical overhead to set up a copying royalty payment
> plan ... I would hope the AMA, in taking the
> initial national leadership in this, could demonstrate
> the feasibility of such an operation....(2)

On 11 August 1967, Passano met with Cummings and again proposed a royalty fee. Cummings repeated that NLM photocopying was fair use and offered to let W & W observe the operation. The company declined the offer, which was repeated at the end of August. During the latter part of September 1967, NLM provided W & W with the photocopy slips of the preceding six months, plus the draft of a controlled sample survey of the NLM interlibrary loan operation. They also pro-vided W & W with a special place in the library to work and monitor the operation.

Nevertheless, on 27 February 1968, W & W filed suit in the U.S. Court of Claims, Washington, D. C., No. 73-68, alleging eight counts of copyright infringe-ment against the U.S. government (National Library of Medicine and the Library of the National Institutes of Health), on the basis that the defendant had violated the law "by copying, printing, reprinting, publishing, vending and distributing said work, all in violation of the plaintiff's rights...."

This case is viewed as important and serious. It is important because it represents a major effort on all sides (librarians, authors, publishers, and so forth) to reconcile modern technology with a 65-year-old copyright law that is badly in need of updating. It is also serious because it is clear, considering that the entire compensation for infringement is $300, that the action by W & W is a test case that could lead to further actions by the plaintiff and other publishers against the defendants or other libraries. Furthermore, it will undoubtedly have an impact on the pending copyright revision bill. Since the implications of the final decision on library service could be serious, it is necessary to review and discuss the case as a key to the reason for this study.

The case, as described by Court of Claims Commissioner James F. Davis in his opinion, raises long-troublesome and much discussed issues of library photocopying of copyrighted materials and requires for resolution the "judgment of Solomon" if not the "dexterity of Houdini."(3)

Since the issues at stake are critical for all libraries, the American Library Association, the Association of Research Libraries, the Medical Library Association, and the American Association of Law Libraries sought and were granted leave to file briefs as *amicae curiae* in support of the defendant. Likewise, the Authors League of America, Inc., and the Association of American Publishers, Inc., were granted permission to file briefs in support of the plaintiff.

The plaintiff (W & W), a major publisher of medical journals and books, publishes 37 journals dealing with various medical specialties. Among these are the four journals in suit:

1. *Medicine*, a bimonthly published since 1922 by W & W for its own benefit and profit for an annual subscription rate of $12.

2. *Journal of Immunology*, the official journal of the American Association of Immunologists (AAI) since 1916, which is published monthly for AAI by the plaintiff. A contract governs the relationship between AAI and the plaintiff on a 50 percent basis for each party.

3. *Gastroenterology*, the official publication of the American Gastroenterological Association (AGA) since 1943, which is published monthly by the plaintiff through a grant on a 50 percent basis.

4. *Pharmacological Reviews*, the publication for the American Society of Pharmacology and Experimental Therapeutics (ASPET) since 1949, a quarterly published by the plaintiff for ASPET on the same above-mentioned basis.

The articles published in these journals are selected from manuscripts submitted to either the plaintiff (W & W) or the appropriate medical society. The four journals are disseminated nationally and internationally in libraries and schools and among physicians and researchers. Subscription rates vary as follows:

Journal	Subscription rate
Medicine	$12.00
Pharmacological Reviews	15.00
Journal of Immunology	22.00[*]
	44.00[†]
Gastroenterology	12.00[*]
	25.00[†]

The revenues are derived mainly from subscriptions, although a small part comes from advertisements. All four journals are copyrighted by the plaintiff, the Williams & Wilkins Company.

The defendants are the National Institutes of Health (NIH) and the National Library of Medicine (NLM). The NIH, the principal medical research organization of the U.S. government, is a group of institutes located on a sizable campus in Bethesda, Maryland. Each institute specializes in a particular medical field and conducts research both intromurally and through grants-in-aid to private individuals and organizations. The NIH employs 12,000, of whom 4,000 are professional scientists and medical doctors. To assist its researchers, the NIH maintains a library of about 150,000 volumes, of which 120,000 are journals (mainly medical) and the rest are books. Although the library is maintained principally for NIH personnel use, it is also open for public use. Among the 3,000 different journals to which the library subscribes are the four journals in question. As a rule, one copy of the original stays in the library and the others circulate among the researchers. The library also

[*] For members of the above-mentioned societies.

[†] For nonmembers

provides a photocopying service to the researchers who, on request, can obtain a copy of an article from any journal in the library, including the four in suit. Usually, copies are requested to assist in research; nevertheless, the library does not require the reason for requests nor does it require the return of the photocopies, which are usually kept by the researchers for future reference. In 1970 the library filled 85,744 requests for journal articles, including the plaintiff's four journals, constituting about 930,000 pages. If, on the average, a journal article is ten pages long, one can say that the NIH library had made about 93,000 photocopies of articles.(4)

The NLM is located on the campus of the National Institutes of Health. Originally the Armed Forces Medical Library, it was transferred by Congress to the Public Health Service and designated as the National Library of Medicine. It declared its purpose to be "to aid the dissemination and exchange of scientific and other information important to the progress of medicine and to the public health...."(5)

The library is a repository of worldwide medical literature and functions as the libraries' library. The NLM interlibrary loan program (see pp. 42-44) is a well known and very successful program whereby the library shares its vast resources with other research libraries here and abroad. Upon request, the NLM will lend books to other libraries. In the case of journals, the loan is usually in the form of a photocopy of the title requested, supplied free of charge and on a no-return basis. In compliance with the General Interlibrary Loan Code and the Gentleman's Agreement, NLM will provide only *one* photocopy per request and will not photocopy an entire journal issue. However, it places a notice in the margin of each photocopy that reads as follows:

In 1968, NLM received from other libraries about
127,000 requests for loans, mostly for journals, of
which about 120,000 were filled by photocopying single
articles from journals, including the plaintiff's journals.

The plaintiff (W & W) alleged that both the NLM
and NIH copied eight articles from the four journals in
suit between 29 September 1967 and 12 January 1968.
The eight articles are specified in Table 4-1.

The copies were made to the following requestors
(all physicians and medical researchers) on the following
dates:

Article number	Date photocopied	Name of requester
1	9/29/67	Beckman
1	10/5/67	Gabor
1	10/19/67	Backman
2	9/29/67	McCallum
3	9/27/67	McEnany
4	9/27/67	McEnany
4	11/13/67	Reynolds
5	9/27/67	McEnany
5	11/13/67	Reynolds
6	9/27/67	McEnany
7	10/12/67	Bird
8	1/11/68	Pitcher
8	12/68	Young

The defendants conceded that both libraries made at
least one photocopy of each of the eight articles
from one or more of the four journals in suit.
The plaintiff, in filing the suit, was seeking "reasonable

TABLE 4-1

Eight Copied Articles From Four Journals in the Williams & Wilkins Law Suit

	Article	Authors	Journal	Volume	Pages	Year
1.	The Genetic Mucopolysaccharidoses	McKusick, Kaplan, Wise, Hanley, Suddarth, Sevick, Maumanee	*Medicine*	44/6	445-483	1965
2.	Supersensitivity and Subsensitivity to Sympathominmetic Amines	Trendelenburg	*Pharmacological Reviews*	15/2	225-276	1963
3.	Detection of Two Antibodies in Single Plasma Cells by the Paired Fluorescence Technique	Hiramoto, Hamlin	*Journal of Immunology*	95/2	214-224	1965
4.	Fluorescent Antibody Staining ...	Wood, Thompson, Goldstein	*Journal of Immunology*	95/2	225-229	1965
5.	Chromatographic Purification of Tetramethylrhodamine-Immune	Cebra, Goldstein	*Journal of Immunology*	95/2	230-245	1965
6.	The Stability of Messenger Ribonucleic Acid in Antibody Synthesis	Lazda, Starr	*Journal of Immunology*	95/2	254-261	1965
7.	The Course of Non Specific Ulcerative Colitis ...	Banks, Korelitz	*Gastroenterology*	32/6	983-1012	1957
8.	Occlusion of the Hepatic Veins in man	Parker	*Medicine*	38/4	369-402	1959

and entire compensation for alleged infringement by the
United States [NIH and NLM] of certain copyrights
in medical journals."(6)   On the other hand, the plaintiff itself asserts that "photocopying is essential and that
it does not want to interfere with it in any way–they
just want to get paid for any photocopying from their
journals."(7)

The defendant and the *amicae curiae* briefs raised a
number of arguments, the high points of which can be
summarized the following sections.

A. The Ownership Issue

The defendant argued that authors of the eight articles
did not assign the ownership of their manuscripts to
the plaintiff (two of the authors testified in the trial
to that effect).   They may at the most have granted
to the plaintiff a license to publish the articles, which,
under no circumstance, substitutes for an express assignment which is required in such instances.(8)   The
plaintiff's ownership and record title of copyright registration on these journals does not necessarily mean that
W & W is the "proprietor" of copyright on these eight
articles, since it has been ruled that the author or his
assign may obtain copyright or may bring suit of copyright infringement.(9)   The plaintiff's copyright on the
said articles is invalid and has no standing in court in
bringing this suit.

The commissioner did not agree with the defendant
on the ownership issue, on the basis that the authors
did not assert

> any interest (legal or equitable) in their respective
> articles. [And that] ... by custom of long standing
> and absent of any written or oral agreement to the
> contrary, authors who submit manuscripts to medical
> journals do so on the implied understanding that the

> publisher will obtain statutory copyright on the journal (and the individual articles therein).(10)

This part of the opinion raises the question of whether the author (rather than the publisher) retains title to his work, even though it is published as a part of a composite on which the publisher holds a blanket copyright. A scientific journal is a collective work which, as a type, evokes discussions regarding copyright protection, because it consists of independent identifiable items that are capable of being copyrighted on their own; nevertheless, publishers of such works may acquire one copyright that covers the several articles contained in any given issue of a journal (that is, blanket coverage).

Under the current law, Section 3 reads as follows:

> Protection of Component Parts of Work Copyrighted; Composite Works or Periodicals.—The copyright provided by this title shall protect all the copyrightable component parts of the work copyrighted, and all matter therein in which copyright is already subsisting, but without extending the duration or scope of such copyright. The copyright upon composite works or periodicals shall give to the proprietor thereof all the rights in respect thereto which he would have if each part were individually copyrighted under this title.

The law, therefore, gives the proprietor (that is, the publisher of a collective work) the right to acquire a copyright for the whole work, which is equal to securing a separate copyright on each independant article within the work. This is also confirmed in practice as authors, particularly in scientific and technological fields, are known to be more concerned with publishing their work than protecting it. The controversy emanates, however, from the fact that many authors are not aware of their rights when they submit their manuscripts for publication. Subsequently, the publisher, in an attempt to protect his investment, applies for a copyright without the proper intention and/or assignment of the author. The problem is further complicated because, as it stands now, the copyright on a collective work is considered an "indivisible entity" that can be transferred only as a whole. The issue, therefore, can be seen in three situations:

1. The author assigns his rights to the publisher and the publisher applies for the copyright on the whole collective work, in which case each single article is protected.

2. The author retains any right to his article, whereby the publisher cannot acquire copyright on it. In the meantime, the copyright on the collective work does not protect the article, which will result in its being published without the proper copyright notice and inadvertently falling in the public domain.

3. The author applies and obtains a copyright to his article before it is published in the collective work, in which case he must make sure that a separate copyright notice appears on his own article; otherwise, it would be considered a case of publication without proper copyright notice, which will result, unintentionally, in its falling into the public domain.

The proposed revision bill S.1361 defines a collective work as follows:

> Section 101: A "collective work" is a work such as a periodical issue, anthology, or encyclopedia, in which a number of contributions, constituting separate and independent works in themselves, are assembled into a collective whole.

This leads to the distinction between "collective work" and "joint work" such as a musical production in which the several contributions (for example, text, music, and choreography) would be copyrighted separately and would be joined together to produce one production.

The bill, in general, does not change the existing rights in collective works; however, it clarifies the situation in which the author in a collective work retains the rights to his contribution. This clarification is in Section 201 (c) of the bill which indicates that:

> the copyright in a collective work is distinct from the copyright in an individual contribution to that work; and

> the copyright for each separate contribution will initially invest in the author of that contribution

The author's copyright, therefore, will be preserved even when his contribution is published as part of a collective work without a proper copyright notice.

Journal publishers naturally are not in favor of this proposed provision since the copyright in the collective work would not grant them an exclusive right on all its components.

> Nothing in this title shall be construed to annul or limit the right of the author or proprietor of an unpublished work, at common law or in equity, to prevent the copying, publication, or use of such unpublished work without his consent, and to obtain damages thereafter.

The author is the sole owner of the common literary property on his work. This being so, he may choose one of the following avenues:

1. He may print his work in a restricted and limited number and never allow it to be published and sold to the public, in which case he retains his rights indefinitely.

2. He may grant permission for a "general publication," at which time his common law rights cease to exist. In this case he has to either (a) apply and obtain, in his own name or by assigning his rights in full to a proprietor, a statutory copyright on the work; or (b) not apply and let his work fall in the public domain.

In the absence of such assignment one may say that the W & W has an invalid copyright on the eight articles, which, therefore, can be considered in the public domain.

On the other hand, the absence of any evidence to the contrary may be also construed, in conjunction with the submission of the manuscript to the publisher without restriction, as a transfer of all the author's rights, title, and interest in the work, including his copyright.(11)

However, Dr. Victor McKusick, author of an article in *Medicine* and a witness for NIH and NLM, testified that his article "was written to disseminate information concerning the particular ... area that I have been working in."(12) He also added that "research without communication is useless." In the absence of any evidence to the contrary, a nonrestrictive customary transfer of the manuscript is more likely to mean dedication rather than assignment of the literary property in work.

B.   The Infringement Issue

The defendant contended that the NIH and NLM
acts of copying "do not violate the copyright owner's
exclusive right 'to copy' the copyrighted work provided
by Title 17 U.S. Code Section 1" on the basis that
making single copies "is not, in itself, sufficient to incur
liability" and that the actionable copying must include
printing and publishing of multiple copies of the copyrighted work.

In his report, the commissioner stated that the 1909
copyright act eliminated the distinction between "copying,"
"printing," and "publishing" and that under the present
law any of these acts constitute a violation of the
owner's copyright.   He added that libraries in general
may make one copy per request, but they do that over
and over again.   This is analogous to the fact, quoting
Sophar and Heilprin, that "babies are still born one at
a time, but the world is rapidly being overpopulated."
(13)   Furthermore, the 1790 statute considers it an
infringement to make "any copy or copies" of a
copyrighted work (Section 2), and nothing in the subsequent statutes suggests a change in that concept.

Shaw, in his analysis of the case, differs with
the commissioner in that Title 17, U.S. Code, Section
107, which deals with importation, during copyright,
of copyrighted books, and so forth, recognizes single
copies and private use as well as the right to use an
agent (for example, a library) to make single copies for
the private use of scholars.(14)   The scholar, therefore,
has the right to make a copy or import a copy for
his private use, and what he can do for himself he can
do through an agent.

There is a basic difference between "public use"
and "private use."   The method of reproducing single
or multiple copies in relation to either purpose is not

necessarily significant. Making one copy of a music sheet for public use, for example, is a violation of the author's right.   The method of copying and the number of copies do not determine whether it is a violation.

C. The Fair Use Concept

The defendant also contended that its copying is a fair use of copyrighted works, as described by the judically created doctrine.   The plaintiff refuted this defense on the basis of the principle *de minimis non curat lex** or, as W & W puts it, "[fair use] comes into play only when a relatively small amount of copying takes place."

The commissioner, however, described the defendant's practice as "wholesale copying" and said that it meets none of the criteria for fair use because: (a) the photocopies are exact duplicates of the original articles; (b) they are intended to serve as a substitute for the original articles; and (c) they serve to diminish the plaintiff's potential market since the copies are made at the request and for the benefit of a potential subscriber to the plaintiff's journals.(15)

The defendant argued that there is no evidence that unauthorized photocopying has harmed the plaintiff.   It also said that the photocopying by NIH and NLM is "reasonable and customary" and is consistent with the terms of the Gentleman's Agreement.   The defendant also noted that NLM has a statutory duty to make available "through loans, photographic and other copying procedures" such materials in the library as the Secretary of Health, Education and Welfare deems appropriate.   In addition, there are statutory grants to medical libraries

*The principle means "the law does not notice, or care for, small trifling matters."

for the acquisition of duplicating devices, which suggests that Congress intended to exempt NLM and other medical libraries from the copyright law.(16)

The commissioner, in reply, stated:

> The [gentleman's] agreement was drafted on behalf of a book publisher's organization which is now defunct and to which the plaintiff [W & W] never belonged. In fact, ... no periodical publishers were represented in the organization at the time [1935] the "agreement" was drafted; and consequently the agreement cannot speak of their interests or problems.(17)

He concluded that "the doctrine of 'fair use' and the 'Gentleman's Agreement' ... cannot support wholesale copying of the kind here in suit."(18)

Shaw, in his previously mentioned analysis, indicated that the copyright act has nothing to do with the "private use" of copyrighted material by scholars in its original or copy form. He was also of the opinion that

> the Constitution authorized the Congress to pass a Copyright Act, giving authors and their assigns a monopoly of *general public uses* for limited periods.... Title 17 U.S. Code ... in itself and its interpretations and in constitutional intent, deals solely with general public use.(19)

One can say, therefore, that it is the character of the reader's use of the copied work that determines the issue of fair use versus infringement. The reader's use does not change whether copying is manual or mechanical or whether the reader makes the copy himself or asks the library to do it for him.

One of the many points raised by the defendant deserves mention. The defendant called the court's attention to the fact that articles 1, 4, 5, and 6 (See Table 1) state on their opening pages that "the research work therein reported was supported, at least in part, by grants from the defendant's Public Health Service." The commissioner, however refuted the argument on the basis that the funds were granted prior to 1 July 1965, at which time the policy of the Public Health Service did not reserve the government any rights in copyrighted publications enumerating grant-funded research.

Finally the commissioner stated:

> What the defendant really appears to be saying is that the copyright law *should* excuse libraries from liability for the kind of copying here in suit. That of course is a matter for Congress, not the courts, to consider for it involves questions of public policy aptly suited to the legislative process.(20)

The commissioner of the Court of Claims concluded his report by recommending that the Williams & Wilkins Company is entitled to recover from the NIH and NLM reasonable and entire compensation for infringement of copyright.

The report was filed on 16 February 1972 and within 90 days, as required by law, the U.S. government appealed the case before the entire Court of Claims. On 27 November 1973, the court, in what is described as a "groundbreaking" case, reversed the holding with a finding of no infringement liability by the defendant on the basis that the NIH and NLM photocopying practice constitutes a fair use.(21) The court split 4 to 3 in overturning a trial judge's opinion that would have barred such photocopying by libraries, schools, researchers, and students. In deciding on the case, the court addressed two main issues. The first concerned the question of whether the 1909 copyright act applies to "copying" of books and journals, thus supporting the "infringement" issue in suit.   The second, and major, question was the balancing of equities in deciding whether the photocopying by the defendant libraries was "fair" or "unfair" use. The ruling of the court concerning the infringement issue is followed by a discussion of the fair use issue.

In ruling on the infringement issue, the court noted that an analysis of the copyright acts from 1790 to 1909 produced the finding that the early statutes distinguished "copying" from "printing," "reprinting," and "publishing."   These acts provided that the copyright protection for books is infringed only by "printing," "reprinting," and "publishing."   Despite the fact that the 1909 act obliterated any such distinction between the various practices, the defendant libraries claimed that the legislative history of the 1909 act should be maintained with the proscription against "copying" not being applied to books or journals.   The majority felt that this argument, although not dispositive of the case, at least raised a "solid doubt" and should be taken into account.[*](22)

Concerning the fair use issue, the court held that since the plaintiff did not show that the defendant's use was "unfair," the photocopying by NIH and NLM should be designated "fair use."   This finding was premised on a balancing of three tenets:

1. The plaintiff (W & W) did not show substantial harm by the defendant's photocopying practices.

---

[*]One of the reasons for the majority feeling is the fact that the Librarian of Congress at that time, Herbert Putnam, allowed photoduplication of copyrighted works before and after the 1909 act.   Since he was the major proponent of the act and was intimately involved in its preparation, the majority of the court felt that this was an indication of Congress' approval of photocopying.

The defendant libraries are scientific, non-profit institutions and their objectives and functions are untainted by any commercial gain. The copying in question, therefore, is lawful because it is for scientific use.
In addition, the majority stated that the primary concern is how the copies were used not how many copies were made.

2. The court contended that

> there is no doubt in our minds that medical science would be seriously hurt if such library photocopying were stopped.... This proposition ... is admitted by plaintiff and conceded on all sides.(23)

The court documented this contention by referring to trial testimony showing that the infeasibility of alternatives to photocopying the eight articles was due to an inadequate supply of reprints and back issues and unwillingness or inability of libraries to subscribe to journals which will be used only occasionally. Thus, the court concluded that a judgment for the plaintiff (W & W) would cause scientists to simply do without many of the desired and needed articles for their work.

3. Since the balance between accommodating the interests of science and accommodating those of publishers is one necessitating legislative guidance and solution, the court would not put such a risk of harm on science and medicine during the period before congressional action.(24) The majority claimed that since this cause of action was under the 1909 act, which gave no directives concerning photoduplication and fair use, the problem is one of

containing, such mediating social, economic, and
policy factors so as to necessitate congressional
action.   As a result the majority felt that a
judgment for the plaintiff was precluded as being
"legislative in nature"(25) and that it is up to
Congress to draw the hard line between "fair"
and "unfair" use.   In dissenting opinion, Judge
Philip Nicholas, Jr., predicted that the ruling
"will encourage unrestricted piracy" of all
author's works.   "However hedged," Nicholas
stated, "the decision will be read that a copyright holder has no rights that a library is
bound to respect.   We are making the Dred
Scott decision of copyright law."(26)

On 20 February 1974, the lawyers for W & W
appealed the case to the U.S. Supreme Court and on
May 28 the Court agreed to hear the case which was
decided on 25 February 1975.

The defendant had, and there is no reason to
believe that he would not continue to have, the support
of several library associations (for example, the American
Library Association, the Association of Research Libraries,
and the American Association of Law Libraries), which
have submitted to the commissioner and the full bench
of the Court of Claims *amici curiae* outlining the
critical issues at stake for libraries in general and the
relevance of the case to practices common throughout
the library world.   Emphasis was put on the importance
of the court's final decision to the future of libraries
and research activities in addition to its long-range impact
on the advancement of learning and knowledge in the
United States.

It is interesting to note that early in March 1972,
two weeks after the commissioner filed his report,
W & W sent a digest of the opinion to its subscribers

and proposed a "reasonable annual license fee" in lieu of an itemized royalty payment. Shortly thereafter, the publisher's customers were informed that "institutional rates" would be enforced for 1973 subscriptions, raising the price of journals an average of $3.65. A leaflet entitled "Instructions for Photocopying" informed subscribers that the increase included "an automatic license to make single-copy photocopies for library patrons in the regular course of library operations" but not for library loans, which "may be made upon remittance of five cents per page per copy made."(27)

On 23 June 1972, the NLM and its regional medical librarians were informed by W & W that they would be assessed the institutional rate allowing them in-house photocopying and should expect to pay the publisher five cents per page royalty for any interlibrary loan copying.

While disagreeing with the five cent per page royalty, Cummings, on June 31, agreed to the increase in subscription charges providing that it was not to be construed as a licensing to NLM's photocopying. Two months later, W & W conceded and retracted the licensing implication while court action was pending and agreed, in the meantime, not to implement its proposal on compensation for interlibrary loan photocopying.

A few publishers (for example, Marcel Dekker, Inc., and Pergamon Press) joined W & W in proposing the "institutional rates" to their subscribing libraries. This move confirms the prediction regarding the serious effect of the court decision on libraries and the scientific world. The situation can best be described in the register of copyright's statement regarding the current stalemate over photocopying in general as "the most dangerous, most difficult and most urgent problem facing the library publishing community today."(28)

NOTES

1. *Libraries and Copyright: A Summary of the Arguments for Library Photocopying.* Chicago: American Library Association, June 1974.

2. *Ibid.,* p. 7.

3. *The Williams & Wilkins Company* v. *The United States.* The United States Government of Claims, Report of Commissioner James F. Davis to the Court, No. 73-68, Feb. 16, 1972, p. 2.

4. *Ibid.,* p. 4.

5. 24 United States Code. Section 274, 1970.

6. *The Williams & Wilkins Company* v. *The United States.* *op. cit.,* p. 32.

7. R. R. Shaw, "Williams & Wilkins v. the United States." *American Libraries* 3: 988 (Oct. 1972).

8. *Morse* v. *Fields.* 127 F. Supp. 63, 65, 104 USPQ 54, 55 (S.D. N.Y. 1954).

9. *Kinelow Publishing Co.* v. *Photography-in-Business, Inc.* 270 F. Supp. 851, 155 USPQ 342 (S.D. N.Y. 1967).

10. *The Williams & Wilkins Company* v. *The United States.* *op. cit.,* p. 8.

11. *Geisel* v. *Poynter Production, Inc.,* 205 F. Supp. 331, 160 USPQ 590 (S.D. N.Y. 1968).

12. *The Williams & Wilkins Company* v. *The United States.* U.S. Court of Claims, No. 73-68, Court Record, p. 66.

13. Gerald J. Sophar and Lawrance B. Heilprin, *The Determination of Legal Facts and Economic Guideposts with Respect to the Dissemination of Scientific and Educational Information as It is Affected by Copyright–A Status Report.* Prepared under Project 7-0793, Contract OEC-1-7-070793-3559 for Bureau of

Research, Office of Education, Department of Health, Education and Welfare, Dec. 1967, p. 16.

14. Shaw, *op. cit.*, p. 997.

15. *The Williams & Wilkins Company* v. *The United States.* *op. cit.*, p. 16.

16. *Ibid.*, p. 19.

17. *Ibid.*, p. 19.

18. *Ibid.*, p. 21.

19. Shaw, *op. cit.*, p. 999.

20. *The Williams & Wilkins Company* v. *The United States.* *op. cit.*

21. *The Williams & Wilkins Company* v. *The United States.* The United States Court of Claims, No. 73-68, decided Nov. 27, 1973.

22. *Ibid.*, p. 9.

23. *Ibid.*, p. 19.

24. *Ibid.*, p. 25.

25. *Ibid.*, p. 29.

26. *Ibid.*, p. 69.

27. *Libraries and Copyright: A Summary of Arguments for Library Photocopying.*   Chicago: American Library Association, June 1974, p. 7.

28. *Ibid.*, p. 2.

Chapter 5

THE ECONOMICS OF PUBLISHING

Is copyright an incentive for the creation of new works which would not have been created in the absence of a copyright system? Some believe that literary publications will decrease or almost disappear if copyright protection is abolished. To examine this assumption one has to view it in relation to the two beneficiaries of any copyright system: the author and his assign, the publisher. The reason is that their degree of dependence on copyright differs. Copyright may encourage an author to write because he can expect to be paid for and collect royalties from his copyrighted work. But there are those who create because of expectations other than monopoly profits. Some authors, for example, write without any intention of publishing the ideas they have committed to paper.(1) Some write mainly to advocate certain ideas, or to acquire recognition, or to build a reputation, or simply out of the notion of altruism. Others may write to meet certain requirements of productivity (as in academe) or simply because they like to write. In fact, some authors actually pay part or all the costs of publishing their works. On the other hand, most publishers, other than those involved in religious and partisan works, are in business for profit. A publisher's work can be classified as an entrepreneurial function, which does not necessarily require a major capital (for example, the average capital for a moderate publishing house is estimated at $100,000).(2)

A publisher's activities are almost always contractual; he contracts with the author to write, with the printer to print, and likewise with the binder, the book dealer, and so forth.   A publisher's capital, in essence, is not tied up in major or physical equipment.   The industry, however, is extremely competitive and entry into it is so easy and free that it is called the "Adam Smith's kind of industry."(3)   It is because of this "openness" that copyright protection is a necessity.   In the absence of copyright, a competitor can copy an already published work and avoid the costs of royalties, editing, and so forth.   Consequently, he can market the copied edition at a price below the cost of the initial publisher, who will accordingly suffer a financial loss.   Statutory copyright is therefore more of a necessity to the publisher than to the author of a published work.   The fact that this is not taken into consideration could be blamed on the legislators' unsatisfactory approach to the problems of monopoly in copyright whereby "they treat copyright as protection for the author rather than protection for the publisher, which in fact is its primary function."(4)

Publishers fall into three categories: (a) book publishers, (b) journal publishers, and (c) book and journal publishers.   Scientific and technical information is usually contained in one of three types of journals:

1. *Primary journals*, which record textual information and serve as a current awareness tool

2. *Secondary journals*, which abstract and index the information appearing in primary journals

3. *Tertiary journals*, which review and evaluate the information published in primary journals.

Each of these types of journals has its own characteristics, market, and problems.   This study is concerned
mainly with primary journals.

In contrast to book publishing, little research has
been done in journal publishing due to the overwhelming
diversity of the economics, contents, and subscribers
support of journals.   For example, there are large
journals that publish about 500 times as much per year
as small journals, considering bulk alone.   The spread in
price is also diverse; some "best buys" in 1968 provided
90 times as many words per penny as the "worst
buy."(5)   Journals published by societies are usually
cheaper than those published as a profit-making venture.
Circulation varies greatly, several factors being (a) the
number of people (scientists, researchers, and so forth)
in the general field of the journal that constitutes the
market for it and (b) the quality, price, and reputation
of the journal.

It is not the intention of this study to survey or
investigate the economics of journal publishing in *all*
fields of science and technology.   The study, in this
respect, makes use of and refers to the extensive and
valuable report, "Task Group on the Economics of
Primary Publication"(known as the SATCOM report), by
the Committee on Scientific and Technical Communication (National Science Foundation, 1970) as well as an
unpublished doctoral dissertation, "Structure, Behavior and
Performance in the Scientific Journal Market" (Yale
University, 1970), which was supplied to the writer
through the courtesy of the author, Sanford V. Berg.

Journals are the "life blood of research" or, as
Victor McKusick, one of the witnesses in *The Williams
& Wilkins Company* v. *the United States,* put it,
"Research without communication is useless," not only
in terms of making one's own results available but in
terms of "consulting the prior literature."(6)   In this

respect, the value of a scientific journal is not measured by the cost of producing the journal but rather by its social value, which comprises its value to subscribers in addition to its value to others and to future generations. However, the price that a potential subscriber is willing to pay for a journal usually represents the value of this journal to him; this, of course, varies from one person to another. Also, the time people are willing to invest in reading journals varies from one field of knowledge to another and may have a dollar value many times larger than the production cost of the journal itself. Despite all these variables, the cost of producing the journal is a major factor in its subscription rate.

First, one has to differentiate between the different types of publishers of scientific journals.

1. *Scientific societies:* Journals so published are less expensive than those issued by private publishers (almost 0.23 cents per kiloword[*]). This is due to page charges or subsidies from the society dues.

2. *Nonprofit organizations:* University presses are a good example of this category. Journals published by them tend to be average in price.

3. *Corporations and government agencies:* The journals published usually report the projects of the publisher. Since such journals are heavily subsidized, they also tend to be inexpensive.

4. *Private publishers:* These are commercial enterprises that are in business to make a profit. This objective, in addition to the lack of subsidies, tends to result in more expensive journals

[*]A kiloword is 1,000 words.

than those in any of the above-mentioned categories (almost 1.5 cents per kiloword).(7)

In addition to the price and quality of the contents
of the journal, circulation is an important influencing
factor in all four categories of journal publishing. Circulation in turn is dependent on many factors, individual
and financial, the most important of which is the number of people (potential subscribers) in the general field
of the journal. The SATCOM report shows that the
average rate of manpower growth in science and technology is about four percent a year. Hypothetically,
the circulation of the journals in any given field of
knowledge should therefore increase four percent annually. This is not necessarily true for several reasons
that will be discussed later in this chapter.

An average circulation figure is usually less than
15,000 per year. Journals in very few fields have a
circulation above that figure. A circulation of 50,000
or more occurs in a small number of medical journals,
especially those with a clinical orientation.(8) Relatively few journals have a circulation below 1,500 (for
example, biology). One has to bear in mind, however,
that these figures reflect the total circulation, including
subscriptions that are offered to society members at a
reduced rate which is usually a part of their annual
dues.

The cost of production is a major factor in the
economic picture of any journal. To understand the
makeup of the cost, one has to break down production
to its simplest elements. This can be accomplished by
arranging those elements in three columns by logical
status and in several rows by geographical location
(organizational entities) and chronological sequence,
starting with "technical editing" and ending with "mailing" (see Figure 5-1). As shown in Figure 5-1,

FIGURE 5-1.   Costs of Journal Production (Adapted from the SATCOM Report).

Location	Prerun costs	Miscellaneous costs	Runoff costs
Editor's office*	Technical editing Referees Editors Clerks Telephone, postage, etc.		

Production office*	Copy editing
	Copy editors
	Clerks
	Art department
	Indexes
	Proofreading
	Page-charge billing
	Typewriter composition
		Promotion
		Advertising
		Solicitation and
		  correspondence
		Processing of copy
		Handling of reprints
		  and back issues
			Subscription
			  maintenance

Engraver	Engravings		

Printer	Composition
	Typesetting
	Proofreading
		Back issues:
		  Overrun for issues
		  Reprints
		  Mailing
			Printing
			Paper
			Presswork
			Binding
			Wrapping and mailing

*Editors and production staff sometimes operate together. Overhead expenses, such as rent, utilities, etc., and employees benefits should be included.

logical sequence of production consists of prerun costs, miscellaneous costs, and runoff costs. Each of these will be discussed separately.

A. Prerun Costs

This part consists of all the necessary operations needed *before* the production of the first copy of the printed work. The cost of all the prerun elements, as a rule, is independent of the number of copies produced of any given journal. The prerun consists of the following elements.

1. Technical Editing

Every science and technology journal has one or more technical editors who are usually highly trained professionals in the field of the journal. According to the SATCOM report, the salaries of full-time technical editors may vary from below $12,000 for a junior scientist ... to over $40,000 for a "big name."(9) Costs of technical editing also include salaries for a clerk or semitechnical assistant (from $4,000 to $10,000). Costs in this element of production should be augmented by about ten percent for employee benefits and by approximately $1,500 per man-year for the cost of office space and other institutional services (for example, library facilities, plus a small amount of money for office supplies, telephone, postage, and so forth.)(10) However, in science and technology journals, technical editing is commonly a part-time activity of a scientist employed by a university or a research laboratory. In this case, the journal pays some sort of stipend to the editor, plus certain office expenses such as for the telephone, the mail, and sometimes the salary of a secretary. The stipend varies from higher percentages for university presses to lower percentages for commercial presses. The average compensation, however, is around $3,000 per ten published kilowords.(11) These payments usually never make allowance for the value of space and some other overhead items. In fact, the editor's stipend usually does not cover the true value of the time he spends on the journal. He usually does not charge the journal for the time he spends attending conferences, reading, or talking with his colleagues. These activities, which are necessary to preserve his competence in his field, are estimated at 20 percent of his time.(12) It is fair to say that the employer of the part-time editor is really subsidizing the journal. In the economics of journal publishing these types of costs for technical editing are known as "hidden or unaccounted for costs."(13) With the above-mentioned hidden or unaccounted for costs, the SATCOM report estimated, with a hypothetical editor's salary of $25,000 and a clerk's salary or $5,000, that technical editing in general costs about $10.75 per kiloword.(14)

Technical editing also includes refereeing, which is usually done on a voluntary basis. Although they donate their services, referees are paid an honorarium by some commercial publishers. Their job is mainly to evaluate the manuscript considered for inclusion in the journal. Since journal publishers do not keep a record of the time spent by referees, it is hard to make a dollar estimate of the cost of refereeing per paper. It is important to note, however, that some highly specialized journals do much of the evaluation through editors and less through referees. On the other hand, large prestigious journals submit all papers to referees. In this case, referring activities and costs contribute to the true cost as much as technical editing.

2. Copy editing

This includes the preparation of manuscripts for the typesetter or other compositors by copyeditors who usually have certain skills but not necessarily a thorough knowledge of the scientific or technical field of the journal. This "editorial mechanics" operation includes marking the manuscripts for the typesetter, standardizing the headings, styling the footnotes, planning the layout of the figures, and some proofreading. Copyediting usually takes place at the journal production office; nevertheless, some of it may be done at the technical editor's office or even at the printer's workshop. In Beisel's study of the American Institute of Physics, the 1967 cost of copyediting for a number of scientific and technical journals was found to range from $7.50 to over $28 per kiloword, with a general average of $12 to $16. The variation is due partly to variations in the work efficiency (for example, large-scale operations maintain a more uniform work load) and partly to variations in the difficulty of the processed material.

3. Composition

Composition is the final stage of producing the journal in its physical form. This can be accomplished through typesetting or the photo-offset method, which utilizes a special typewriter. Composition costs differ markedly, depending on the method used and the difficulty of the text being set, from one compositor (printer) to another. The total costs of composition usually also include the costs of proofreading, corrections, and engravings, if any are used. As indicated in the SATCOM report, the total composition costs range from $20 per kiloword for pure nonsymbolic text to $60 for mathematical materials. The average cost is $30 to $40 per thousand words.(15)

It is interesting to note that photo-offset is about one-third cheaper than regular typesetting. This is due to the lesser time involved in photocomposition, in making corrections, and in the preparation of figures, which is done by paste-in rather than by the method used with engravings.

B. Miscellaneous Activities

Miscellaneous activities are those parts of production containing incidental rather than necessary operations. These may include promotional activities for the journal, the solicitation of advertisements, and the handling of reprints, back issues, and correspondence. The activities involved in this part of production are regarded as "independently desirable" for the well-being of the journal, and they can be made to yield, directly or indirectly, more income than they cost.

C. Runoff Costs

This part of the production activity handles the dissemination of the journal as a final product. The runoff costs cover paper, printing, postage, binding, maintenance of records, and sample copies.

The costs of paper, printing, and postage are, in this instance, proportionate with the amount of material printed. While a recent practice is to mail the journal without the wrapping, the cost of binding (covers), wrapping, and mailing corresponds to the number of issues mailed. The cost of maintaining subscriber information records corresponds to the number of subscribers. A last cost is that for unusable copies and excess copies for sample purposes.

To cover all these costs (prerun, miscellaneous, and runoff), a publisher has to have several sources of income to balance his expenses if he is a publisher of a nonprofit journal or to balance the costs and recognize a profit if he is a commercial publisher. Subscriptions are the biggest source of income for most scientific journals. However, many scientific and technical journals derive additional income from the following sources:

1. Page Charges

Page charges are certain sums of money per published page of any article. The charges are requested from the author upon submission of his report for publication. Usually the grantor or supporter (that is, institute, society, government, or foundation) of the reported research covers the page charges.

Page charges originated in the American Institute of Physics and have spread recently to almost all fields of science and technology. The majority of scientific journals requesting page charges are published by scientific societies; however, about six percent of commercial publishers of journals impose such fees. The range of page charges varies with the size of the published page, so that large pages cost more than smaller ones. The variation also extends to the basis for the charges. Some journals charge for every page (for example, in *Physics*) and some charge for pages beyond a certain number.*

In practice, the payment of the requested page charges has no bearing on the decision to publish a

---

*For example, the *Journal of Immunology*, which is published by the Williams & Wilkins Company, charges $40 per page in excess of six pages in any given article.

paper. "Accepted papers whose sponsors decline to pay
the page charges are published anyway."(16)　Page
charges, however, are honored since the 1961 policy
statement of the Federal Council of Science and Technology considered it legitimate to charge for the publication of any research work sponsored by the government.

2. Subsidies

Subsidies come from the associations or institutions
that publish the journal. One has to bear in mind,
however, that the majority of scientific and technical
journals published by societies are usually sold to society
members at a lower subscription rate. Moreover, in
some cases, the member receives the journal free of
charge as a part of his membership. This is conceivable in small associations; nevertheless, bigger associations
usually give their members a choice of subscribing to
any of the association's journals. (For example, the
annual dues for membership in the American Library
Association entitle the members to receive *American
Libraries* without further cost. Any additional desired
publications for the several divisions of ALA have to
be paid for.) The SATCOM report estimated that
association subsidies to scientific and technical journals
vary from "negligible amounts to 30 percent or more
of the total production cost."(17)

3. Advertisements

Advertisements are another important source of
income, particularly for journals of large circulation.
In Campbell and Edmisten's study,(18) 52 percent of
the journals carried some advertising, and about one-
tenth of all association journals, and one-fifth of

commercial journals, received no more than ten percent
of their income from advertising.   In general, any of
these journals must devote on the average of five to ten
percent of its pages to advertisement to be able to acquire that percentage of income.   However, space allo-
cated for advertisement depends on the size of the
journal's circulation.   The SATCOM study reported that,
in the 5,000 to 10,000 circulation group, 4 out of 21
journals devoted more than five percent of their space
to advertisement.   The same percentage on both counts
was true of journals in the 10,000 to 20,000 circulation
range.   Journals with circulation above 20,000 usually
have as much text as advertisements in any issue and
are able to acquire from advertisements sufficient funds
to cover 50 to 75 percent of their production cost.
Scientific news journals (for example, the *Journal of the
American Medical Association, Scientific Research,* and
Physics Today) allocate space for advertisement equal to
the space assigned to news and materials.(19)

4. Reprints and Back Issues

Reprints and back issues constitute a very small part
of the journal's income and may net, on the average,
two to four percent of the total income.   In some
exceptional cases, particularly in biomedicine, the value
may rise to 10 to 20 percent of the total income.
It is apparent that back issues are more valuable and
render more income in commercial publishing than in
society publishing because the charge and the need for
back issues are higher in the former's market.

5. Royalties

Royalties may yield very little or no income to
scientific journals.   The chances are minimal that the

copyright owner is able, as it stands, to count on a
sizable or meaningful income from licensing others to use
the published material.   This is the controversial issue
that is raised by the publishing industry.

6. Subscriptions

Subscriptions are a major source of income for
scientific and technical journals.   The subscription rate
is based on the cost and the number of subscribers.
In the last decade, the rise in subscription rates has
become a fact of life.   The price indexes for U.S.
periodicals in all fields of knowledge from 1958 to
1968 have increased by a factor 1.76 and those in
chemistry, and physics in particular, have increased by
a factor 2.42.(20)   The percentage of increase has continued to rise along with the annual price.   Using
Library Journal's annual reports on price indexes of
periodicals and serials,(21) one can observe the trend in
the rising price of periodicals.   These reports are based
on the definition that a periodical is

> a publication which constitutes one issue in a con-
> tinuous series under the same title, published more
> than twice a year over an indefinite period; individual
> issues in the series being numbered consecutively or
> each issue being dated; with newspapers being excluded.

The reports are also based on U.S. periodicals and on
U.S. currency.   According to these reports, the annual
average price and price indexes for all U.S. periodicals
in general and medical periodicals in particular, from
1967 to 1973, are as shown in Table 5-1
Price policies regarding scientific and technical
journals follow the purpose and objectives of any given
publication and its publisher.   Since there are three
types of publishing, pricing a journal can be established

TABLE 5-1

Rise In Price Of All U.S. Periodicals And Medical Periodicals

Year	Number of periodicals	Average price (dollars)	Index Price
	All U.S. periodicals(a)		
1967 to 1969	6,944	8.66	100.0(b)
1970	2,372	10.41	120.2
1971	2,415	11.66	134.6
1972	2,537	13.23	152.8
1973	2,861	16.20	187.1
1974	2,955	17.71	204.5
	Medical periodicals(c)		
1967 to 1969	516	19.38	100.0
1970	172	23.44	120.9
1971	172	27.00	139.3
1972	172	29.59	152.7
1973	172	33.60	173.4
1974	172	36.31	187.3

(a)Ninety-seven titles dropped; 191 added.

(b)Index of 100.0 equivalent to average price for 1967 to 1969.

(c)No titles dropped and none added.

on one of the following criteria: (a) profit maximization, (b) average cost, and (c) marginal cost.

The first criterion is usually followed by commercial publishers, who are in business for profit.   Scientific associations and university presses usually set the
price of their journals according to the second criterion.
However, scientific societies that are dependent on charges
and subsidies to cover their costs follow the third criterion when pricing their journals.

a. Profit Maximization.   The first pricing policy is based
on maximizing profit ( ), which results from the difference between total revenue (R) and total cost (C):

   $= R - C$

Assuming that the demand function is linear, the
demand curve can be stated as follows:

   $P = a + bQ$ (1)

where a   0 (positive), b $<$ 0 (negative), P is price,
and Q is quantity.

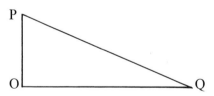

Therefore, total revenue is the price multiplied by the
quantity:

   $R = PQ$ (2)

By substituting Eq. (1) into Eq. (2), one obtains

   $R = \dfrac{(P^2 - aP)}{b}$ (3)

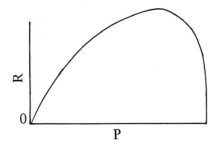

Since the cost curve (C) is in contrast with the demand curve, the former can be expressed as follows:

$$C = F + VQ \qquad\qquad (4)$$

where F　0 (positive), V　0 (positive), F is prerun costs (fixed costs), and V is runoff costs (variable costs).

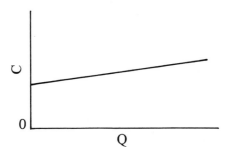

Since P = a + bQ [see Eq. (1)],

$$Q = \frac{P - a}{b}$$

Therefore,

$$C = F + \frac{V(P\text{-}a)}{b}$$

where F and V and a   0 (positive) and b   0 (negative).

$$C = F + \frac{VP}{b} - \frac{Va}{b}$$

$$C = \frac{VP}{b} + F - \frac{Va}{b} \tag{5}$$

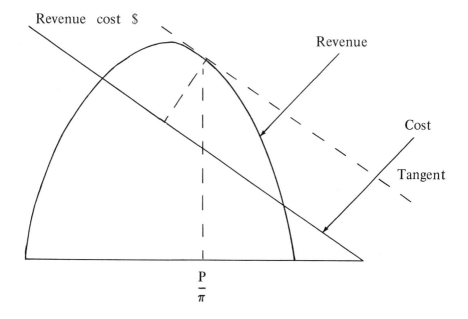

Therefore, by superimposing the revenue curve over the cost curve one can find the point where profits are at a maximum:

The price which yields maximum profit is at the point where a tangent to the revenue curve is parallel with the cost slope, rather than at the top of the revenue curve. Therefore, is the price a commercial publisher should charge to maximize his profits.

Since the slope of the revenue curve (R) is dR/dP (which is the rate of change of the revenue in respect to price) and since

$$R = \frac{P^2 - aP}{b}$$

$$dR/dP = (2P - a)/b$$

and since the slope of the cost curve (C) is dC/dP (which is the rate of change of the cost in respect to price)

$$C = \frac{dC}{dP} = \frac{V}{b}$$

and since the maximum profit is at the point $\overset{P}{-}$ where slope R is equal to slope C, R = C,

$$\frac{2P - a}{b} = \frac{V}{b}$$

$$2P = a + V$$

$$P = \frac{a + V}{2}$$

Therefore

$$\underline{P} = \frac{a + V}{2}$$

b. Average Cost. Scientific societies that publish journals not for profit usually adopt the average cost policy for pricing their journals.

Since $R = PQ$ and $C = F + VQ$, the average cost is at either of the two break-even points.

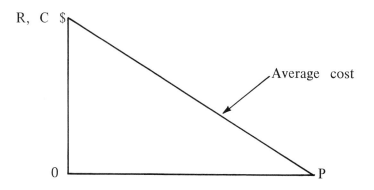

Since the break-even point is $R = C$ and since the average cost is equal to C/Q,

$$PQ = C$$

$$P = \frac{C}{Q} \quad \text{(price = average cost)}$$

$$P = \frac{C}{Q} = \frac{F + VQ}{Q} = \frac{F}{Q} + V$$

and since from Eq. (1)

$$Q = \frac{P - a}{b}$$

then

$$P = \frac{F}{(P - a)/b} + V$$

Therefore average cost pricing is

$$P^2 - AP - VP + Vp + Va - bF = 0 \qquad (7)$$

c. Marginal Cost. Scientific societies that are subsidized and/or ask for page charges usually adopt the marginal cost policy for pricing their journals.

Since marginal cost equals cost of one extra journal equals V, price based on marginal cost is

$$P = V \quad \text{(runoff cost)}$$

and

$$C = F + VQ$$

$$R = VQ$$

In marginal cost pricing (P = V) the publisher loses the prerun cost and bases his price on the runoff cost only. This is possible only if the publisher's prerun cost is subsidized.

Beyond what can be attempted here, using the economics of publishing as a guide, the exact importance of a numerical drop of subscriptions could be assessed in terms of profit maximization as depicted in the previously mentioned diagram. With precise data an investigation would be possible:

1. To determine whether a reduction in the number of subscriptions has an escalator effect so that a

one percent (for example) at some point on the
curve would be of equal importance to a much
larger percent drop on another part of the curve.
The question is whether there is a relation between the reduction in subscriptions and the
reduction in revenue, whereby a slight drop in
subscriptions at a certain point on the revenue
curve would be equally as important as a larger
drop at another point on the same curve. A
one percent drop in subscriptions, for example,
may carry a rather insignificant face value at a
certain point on the curve but may become significant at another point on the same curve
(that is, at the two break-even points; see the
diagram on p. 116). Therefore, although insignificant, one percent may make the difference
between continuing or not continuing publication,
depending on the point where the drop takes
place on the revenue curve. A study of that
nature can be done effectively by investigating
a periodical that ceased publication for economic
reasons. A comparative study and analysis of
the periodical's archives to find out how significant the drop of subscriptions was on the life
of the periodical could render meaningful results
regarding the effect of the drop of subscriptions,
although minimal, on the revenue of specific
points along the curve.

2. To determine if there is a mathematical relationship between reduction in subscriptions and reduction in revenue such that the percentages are
   cumulative and a final small reduction becomes
   completely predictable as a critical factor in the
   economics of publishing. The question here is
   whether there is a relationship with an escalator
   effect between subscriptions and revenue, and

whether this relationship could be expressed as an
algorithm so that the critical points can be
easily predicted. A quadratic equation depicting
the escalating effect of profit/loss on a periodical's revenues can be calculated. For example,
the exact relationship between the drop of subscriptions and its multiplier effect on advertisement revenue could be easily measured and the
critical points compared in relation to subscriptions and revenues.

3. To determine whether there is a critical point
   at which even the slightest drop in the number
   of subscriptions would cause a profit-making publisher to reach a decision to cease publication.
   This is the ultimate result of the above-mentioned
   two assumptions: If there is a relationship between the percentage of drop of subscriptions
   and the revenue, and if this relationship can be
   expressed mathematically, it will be possible to
   find out the point at which the slightest drop
   will make the difference between profit making
   and loss of revenue. In other words, it will be
   possible, by means of regression analysis, to study
   the minimum change that produces the maximum
   effect on the commercial sector of the publishing industry. It is worth noting, in addition,
   that the above-mentioned critical point could be
   well before the break-even point, as the commercial publisher may find it financially unfeasible
   to continue publishing even if he was able to
   cover his prerun and runoff costs.

Nevertheless, the most exact pricing formulas respond
to, but do not control, desired profit margins as costs
increase. For several years prices have, of necessity,

risen.   Paper, composition, and printing costs, plus postal rates, have increased in the last decade faster than the consumer price index.(22)   Page charges and the use of typewritten composition have not helped to keep the price down because the cost of the other elements in production keep rising, the value of the dollar keeps declining because of inflation, and the government con- tinues to cut back on research funds.

Another factor contributing to the increase in sub- scription rates is the bulk of the journal.   Scientific and technical journals, small or large, are getting bigger. The reason is that the flow of information grows stead- ily and each year scientific journals are faced with the dilemma of either expanding in size or rejecting more papers.   Ironically, the end result is the same in both cases.   Publishing more articles adds to the production cost, which results in an increase in subscription rates and in losing some subscribers.   In addition, the in- creasing number of pages in a journal has a reverse psychological effect on the reader who may feel a sense of less value since there may be more that he does not read or use relative to what he did need and use pre- viously.   On the other hand, if a journal decides not to add more pages it will soon hear about the "gaps in the literature" and the "lack of publication outlets," which again may result in losing some subscribers.(23) What happens in most cases is that a new journal will emerge to relieve the pressure on existing journals and to provide an outlet for the increasing output of scien- tists.   The SATCOM report found in 1968, for example, that growth is dominated by commercial publishers at about 8 percent per year, compared to about 1.4 percent for nonprofit journals.(24)   With the growing number and bulk of journals coupled with increasing prices, the user has to be very selective in what he subscribes to because of limitations on budget and time.

It is in this setting that the importance and the effect of library purchases and functions on the publishing of journals becomes obvious. In addition, the volume and extent of library photocopying, as the publishers claim, reduces the number of subscriptions and spreads prerun costs over a smaller number of issues, resulting in pushing the price up, which further reduces the number of subscriptions. The extent of such damage may be significant since library subscriptions are highly important, particularly to journals of low circulation. For instance, a journal selling for $20 per year will be compelled to increase its annual subscription to $22 if it loses 200 out of 2,000 subscribers. The effect of the "burgeoning phenomenon of machine production [of photo-copies]," as Passano of W & W stated, has forced two scientific journals out of existence.

NOTES

1. Robert M. Hurt and Robert Schuchman, "The Economic Rationale of Copyright." *American Economic Review* 61: 425 (May 1966).

2. D. Lacy, "The Economics of Publishing." *Daedalus* 92: 45 (Winter 1963).

3. *Ibid.,* p. 46.

4. L. R. Patterson, "Copyright and the Public Interest." in *Copyright: Current Viewpoints on History, Law, Legislation.* A. Kent and H. Lancour, eds. New York: Bowker, 1972, p. 44.

5. Committe on Scientific and Technical Communication (SATCOM), "Report of the Task Group on the Economics of Primary Publication." Washington D. C.: National Academy of Science, 1970, p. 7.

6. *The Williams & Wilkins Company* v. *The United States.* U.S. Court of Claims, No. 73-68, Court Records, *op. cit.,* p. 666.

7. Committee on Scientific and Technical Communication (SATCOM), *op. cit.*, 52-53.

8. *Ibid.*, p. 58.

9. *Ibid.*, p. 74.

10. *Ibid.*

11. T. H. Campbell and J. Edmisten, *Characteristics of Scientific Journals–1962.* Washington, D.C.: Herner & Co., 1965.

12. Committee on Scientific and Technical Communication (SATCOM), *op. cit.*, p. 76.

13. L. J. Paige [and others]. *A Special Report on the Means of Financing Mathematical Journals.* Providence, R. I.: American Mathematical Society, 1963.

14. Committee on Scientific and Technical Communication (SATCOM), *op. cit.*, p. 76.

15. *Ibid.*, p. 79.

16. *Ibid.*, p. 90.

17. *Ibid.*, p. 95.

18. Campbell and Edmisten, *op. cit.*

19. Committee on Scientific and Technical Communication (SATCOM), *op. cit.*, p. 94.

20. H. W. Tuttle, "Price Indexes for 1968." *Library Journal* 93: 2621-2623 (July 1968).

21. N. B. Brown, "Price Indexes for 1974." *Library Journal* 99: 1775-1779 (July 1974).

22. S. V. Berg, "Structure, Behavior and Performance in the Scientific Journal Market," Ph.D. dissertation. New Haven, Conn.: Yale University, 1970.

23. Joseph H. Kuney, "Economics of Journal Publishing." *American Documentation* 14: 239 (July 1963).

24. Committee on Scientific and Technical Communication (SATCOM), *op. cit.*, pp. 97-93.

Chapter 6

JOURNAL SUBSCRIPTION: A STUDY
OF PHOTOCOPYING

The Williams & Wilkins Company case against the U.S. government emphasized the fact that the four journals *Medicine, Pharmacological Reviews, Journal of Immunology,* and *Gastroenterology* are a good example of highly photocopied scientific journals and could also serve as an example of the library photocopying practice and its effect on journal publishing. The four journals are highly specialized and are published, except for *Medicine* and *Pharmacological Reviews,* in cooperation with the American Association of Immunologists and the American Association of Gastroenterologists. Since the four journals lie mainly within the fields of internal medicine, immunology, gastroenterology, and pharmacology, a stratified sample was selected at random from the practitioners in these fields, and a questionnaire was used to collect the primary data.

The focus of this study centers on the claim that copyright owners of American scientific and technical journals in general, and medical journals in particular, are losing subscriptions due to reprography. This leads to the question of whether reprography is the single most important factor in reducing subscriptions to scientific and technical journals. To test this question it is necessary to show that the loss can be measured and a valid method can be developed to examine the claim regarding the economic impact of reprography on the copyright owners of scientific and technical journals in the United States. This could be done in two steps:

A first step would be to show that medical journals sufficiently represent all scientific and technical periodicals. A second step would be to compare the cost of publishing with expected revenues and to show the effect of photocopying on subscribers' behavior with its further impact on the publishers' revenues. This method would assume the cooperation of publishers and subscribers in the research effort. For reasons explained below, only a portion of the question can be tested at this time.

The main objective of such a study would be to examine the claims of journal publishers. A number of studies have tried to estimate the impact of photocopying on journals. However, the data provided did not determine whether the performance of the potential and/or previous subscriber to scientific and technical journals may have shifted due to the presence of the new technology. The present study was to be conducted in two stages.

The first stage was a survey of the different types of publishers of scientific and technical journals, who were grouped under two broad categories: the profit-making publishers and the not-for-profit publishers. The plan was to send a questionnaire to a sample chosen at random from the two above-mentioned categories of publishers asking for a copy of their current lists of subscribers (November 1970). Another request was to follow in January 1971 asking for a copy of the new lists of subscribers for the new year. The study's intention was to compare the current list with the new list to identify three types of subscribers (individual and/or institutional):

1. Subscribers who dropped their subscriptions for 1971

2. New subscribers for 1971

3. Subscribers who retained their 1970 subscriptions through 1971

Additional information was to be obtained from the two types of publishers through the same questionnaire. The following questions were asked:

1. Are the articles in the journals copyrighted and by whom (author and/or publisher)?

2. Are there any offprints provided for the authors; do the publishers charge for them; do they sell them to readers upon request; for what price; and do they store them against future demand?

In the second stage, a descriptive survey was to be conducted. The three groups of subscribers (individual and/or institutional) would be represented by a random sample and a questionnaire would be sent to acquire the following information:

A. Subscribers Who Dropped or Reduced the Number of Their Subscriptions

Individuals:

1. What is the subscriber's affiliations and subject area?

2. Does he subscribe to any scientific journals, how many, and what are their titles?

3. Was he a subscriber to any of the specific scientific journals (first stage), and for how long?

4. Why did he drop his subscription to any of these journals? Is it because of the availability of reprographic devices or otherwise (lack of interest or funds, change of periodical's policy?

5. If the reason for dropping a subscription is reprography, where did the subscriber make or request his copies, and the amount of material per copy (total periodicals/ article or articles/ in toto or in part)?

6. Does he still read any of these periodicals and by what means?

7. If he does not get his answer from the use of a library collection or from the information center's search, will he consider re-subscribing to any of the periodicals?

8. Can he read all the articles in scientific journals that are relevant in his subject area?

Institutions:

1. Why did the institution drop or reduce the number of its subscriptions to any of the scientific journals (First Stage)? Was it because of the availability or reprographic devices in the specific institution where interlibrary loans are provided in photocopy forms? Or is there any other reason (for instance, no request from users, cut on library or information center's budget, etc.)?

2. What is the institution's policy regarding copying, how much does it charge per page,

and does it provide any single reader with multiple copies of the same item?

3. Is the fee paid by the subscriber equal or greater or less than the search and copying expenses?

B. New Subscribers

Individuals and Institutions:

1. What led them to subscribe to these scientific journals? Was it through the use of reprographic copies? If so, was it over a period of time and how long?

C. Subscribers Who Retained Their Subscriptions

Individuals and Institutions:

1. Do they have access to reprographic devices or copies of these journals other than their own subscriptions? If so, is access to these copies easy or inconvenient? And if it is easy, would they still retain their subscriptions?

2. If the journals are published by an association or society or a university, do they receive them automatically as members of these associations, or do they pay a subscription, other than the association dues, to receive them?

The data from the subscribers who retained their subscriptions would be further analyzed from a 2 x 2 contingency table to estimate the size of the group of subscribers that could be considered a gain to publishers, as in the following example:

If the sample from the population of retained subscribers is 500 and A represents accessibility to reprographic devices or copies, NA represents no access to reprographic devices or copies, B represents membership in association's subscription, and NB represents nonmembership in association's subscription, then

	A	NA	
B	300 60%	100 20%	400
NB	50 10%	50 10%	100
	350	150	500

Thus, the cell NB-A (50) is a proportion of the sample that can be used to estimate the portion of the population that could be considered a gain to publishers, as it represents subscribers who are not members of an association or etc., and in the meantime have access to reprographic devices or copies and still retain their subscriptions.

The economic impact of reprography on subscriptions to scientific journals can thus be determined by comparing the following two formulas:

1. A x B = C

> Where A is the number of subscribers who dropped and/or reduced their subscriptions due to reprography
>
> B is the annual subscription rate of journals in 1971

C is the gross financial loss of subscriptions due to reprography

2. D x B = E

where D is the number of new subscribers who
were introduced to the journals through
reprography

B is the annual subscription rate of journals in 1971

E is the gross financial gain of subscriptions due to reprography

The amount of subscriptions representing the retained
subscribers that are an estimated gain to publishers (see
contingency table on p. 130) is added to the result of
the comparison of the above-mentioned formulas, and a
final conclusion can be drawn from the following for-
mula:

E + F − C = G

where F is the amount of the retained subscriptions
despite the availability of reprographic
devices and copies.

G is the actual gain or loss from scientific
journal subscriptions due to reprography

Since the writer approached several publishing firms
and got negative responses, the study focused on the
four medical journals *Medicine, Pharmacological Review,
Journal of Immunology,* and *Gastroenterology.* The
reason for this choice, as indicated previously, was
because of their representativeness of scientific journals
in the United States in relation to reprography as
practiced by researchers and librarians, a choice that was
strengthened by the fact that these journals were the

subject of litigation in *The Williams & Wilkins Company* v. *the U.S. Government.* Furthermore, other scientific and technical journals, although they have not gone through a test case, have followed the same pattern and have had the same claims as the Williams & Wilkins Company and are waiting for the final decision in the court case, which will certainly have an effect on the entire field of publishing.

Since the representativeness of the four journals in terms of photocopying by researchers and libraries had been established, and since the four journals relate to specific and distinct medical fields, the study's way of finding a suitable population was by determining the main readers of the four journals through means other than the unavailable subscription lists. In searching for the means of predicting the readers that constitute the bulk of the subscribers of these four journals, the writer approached two professional librarians who have specialized in and have been practicing medical librarianship for many years, soliciting their cooperation and help in providing him with a list of the groups that most likely constitute the main users and/or subscribers of the above mentioned journals.

They agreed that the following groups may well constitute the majority of the users that most likely read and subscribe to the four journals: (a) internists, (b) immunologists, (c) allergists, (d) pharmacologists, (e) gastroenterologists, and (f) medical librarians. They also called attention to the fact that the *Journal of Immunology* is a publication of the American Association of Immunologists and that *Gastroenterology* is a publication of the American Association of Gastroenterologists. The members of both associations, therefore, constitute the main readers of these two journals. In addition, they agreed that the membership of the following associations constitute, to a

certain extent, the bulk of the subscribers to the four
journals: (a) the American Board of Internal Medicine,
(b) the American Board of Allergy, (c) the American
Board of Gastroenterology, (d) the American Society of
Pharmacological and Experimental Therapeutics, and (e)
the American Medical Association.

The writer acknowledges the possibility of there being
other types of readers of these journals; however, that the
bulk of subscribers comes from the above-mentioned
groups is a realistic assumption that merits considering
these subscribers as the universe of this study.

A random stratified sample was chosen and the final
sample consisted of the following groups:

	Sample size
Medical librarians	75
Gastroenterologists	133
Pharmacologists	93
Immunologists	116
Internists	369
Allergists	21
Total sample	807

A questionnaire was used as a means for collecting
data needed for this study.   The principal question in
the first section of the questionnaire was divided into
two parts.   The first part asked the person questioned
if he/she subscribed to any of the four journals and
when the subscription started.   This was to help mainly
in dividing the population into two categories: subscribers and nonsubscribers.   The second part was asked if

the questionee had access to any of the four journals
other than through subscriptions. The purpose of this part
was to determine the desire and continuity to subscribe to
any of the four journals despite their availability, free or
for less charge than the subscription rate.

The main question in the second section concerned
the means by which the subscriber was introduced to any
of the four journals. The reason for the question was to
determine if photocopying and/or libraries play a positive
role in gaining new subscribers to these journals.

The question in the third section was directed to that
category of subscribers who dropped or reduced their subscriptions (in case of multiple subscription to one title) to
ascertain the reason for the drop or reduction of subscriptions. The objective was to provide clues as to why
the individual is no longer a subscriber and to determine
if reprography is behind the cutback in subscription.
Other potential reasons were also provided (that is,
budget cost, too much to read, and change in editorial
policy). The individual was asked to check one or more
reasons if applicable.

The question in the fourth section was divided into
two parts. The first was to gather data regarding the
ownership of the copyright on the individual's contributions, if any, to any of the four journals. The purpose was to determine the degree of the author's awareness of their legal rights in their works. The second
part of the question concerned whether offprints of
their works were available to them as authors. The
reason for this part of the question was to provide information about the percentage of availability of offprints
of individual articles in the four journals subject to investigation.

A total of 807 questionnaire was mailed and 343
responses were received which represents approximately
42 percent of the sample. Since medical doctors are

considered among the busiest in any profession and the least interested in filling out questionnaires, the writer was satisfied with the percentage of answers and did not consider sending follow-up letters to the delinquent members of the sample.

Stratified sampling was applied so that there would be no chance of randomly selecting the majority of respondents from one area of medicine. After the percentages that were to be included from each area were determined and after responses to the questionnaire had been tabulated, it was revealed that a comparable percentage from each of the six areas in the sample actually answered the questionnaire. This check ensured that the stratified random sampling was representative of the population.

The following table gives a breakdown by type of respondent and the percentage received from each of these categories:

Type of respondent	Total Number of sample	Number of responses	Percent[a]
Medical librarians	75	51	68
Gastroenterologists	133	69	51
Pharmacologists	93	36	39
Immunologists	116	72	62
Internists	369	106	29
Allergists	21	9	43
Total	807	343	42

[a]It should be noted that all whole numbers are absolute, but percentages are rounded off to the nearest whole percentage.

After all the questionnaires were received, their contents were recorded and counted and percentage figures were assigned to the answers for each group in the sample. The analysis of the data will be discussed in the following chapter.

NOTE

1. "Round Two: Supreme Court Appeal." *American Libraries* 5: 60 (Feb. 1974).

Chapter 7

JOURNAL SUBSCRIPTION: IMPACT
OF PHOTOCOPYING

The question, as stated by Nicholas L. Henry, is "How could we ... promote both the organization and the accessibility of information in a society increasingly permeated by new information?"(1)

The problem is due, in part, to the diverse interests involved in the situation. The author's interest coincides with the publisher's interest, and the user's interest coincides with both. The author writes in order for the publisher to produce and disseminate, and the user must buy if the publisher is to continue to produce and disseminate. Balancing and reconciling these interests is not an easy task.

Since the present 56-year-old copyright law has no provisions regarding the effect of the new technology on copyrighted works, a revision bill was proposed. The bill deals with the current situation and provides provisions covering reprography, computers, and information storage and retrieval systems. The bill revises, among other things, the period of protection and includes, for the first time, the principle of "fair use," a court-made concept, as a part of the new proposed law. The bill, however, is not totally acceptable to all concerned. Much debate, discussion, and testimony were heard. The bill, which passed the Senate, is now pending in the House of Representatives for further discussion and voting.

For some years, commercial publishers, mainly, have been complaining about the escalating infringements on their copyright by researchers, scholars, librarians, and users in general. Their claim is based on the fact that information technologies have advanced, in the past 20 years, in a way which has made it possible for every man to become a publisher. Photocopying, among other technologies, has contributed greatly to this claim. Photocopying is not only an integral part of today's information centers and services, but is becoming almost a second nature to many individuals. Other contributing factors are the continuous cuts in library budgets due to the present economic situation coupled with the new trends in networks and resource sharing. As a result, publishers are complaining about the accelerating decline in sales and the loss of subscriptions due to photocopying. Furthermore, the current copying practice has led some publishers to fear that it may take over the market and force them out of business. This controversy was exemplified in the court case of *The Williams & Wilkins Company* v. *the United States.* The four journals in suit can be considered an exemplification of the actual and potential losses claimed by profit-maximizing publishers of scientific journals. At the time of writing the decision of the Court of Claims (see pp. 91-94) was confirmed by the Supreme Court by a tie vote of four justices, Mr. Blackmun having excused himself from participating. Since the case was a test case, the implications are important and serious. The outcome of the case will have an effect on library service, the use of educational technology, and the individual scientist's and reader's behavior and copying practice. It will also have an effect on the publishing industry.

A. Conclusions

Although the court case represents a phase of the
crisis rather than the substance of it, the basic question
in this study was stated with the understanding that it
might be concerned solely with the claim that copyright
owners of American scientific and technical journals are
losing subscriptions due to reprography.   Investigating
this question would show that the loss can be measured
and a valid research method can be developed to examine the claim of publishers regarding the impact of
photocopying on the copyright owners of these journals.

    Since a complete study of the effect of photocopy-
ing on the publishers of scientific and technical journals
is a greater enterprise than may be undertaken at this
time by one person, the investigator started at the out-
set with the hope that it would be possible to establish a tentative statement that might be tested with the
assumption that the publishers and the subscribers would
cooperate in the research effort.   The turn of events,
however, made it impossible to obtain information from
the publishers, who refused or ignored the writer's requests for data.   Therefore, only a portion of the tentative statement could be tested at the time.

    The study focused on the four medical journals,
Medicine, Pharmacological Reviews, Journal of Immunology,
and *Gastroenterology*, published by the Williams &
Wilkins Company.   The journals were chosen because of
their representativeness of scientific and technical journals
in the United States in relation to reprography as
practiced by researchers and librarians.   The validity of
this choice was also strengthened by the fact that the
four journals were the subject of litigation in the previously mentioned court case.

    Since the Williams & Wilkins Company refused, in
turn, to cooperate with the investigator lest it jeopardize

its standing in the pending case against the government, the study had to be conducted from the standpoint of the subscribers and, therefore, a method had to be developed to determine the bulk of the readership of these four journals through means other than the subscription lists. The membership of specific medical associations and groups were identified and a random sample was chosen with the assumption that these groups constitute the majority of the users that most likely read and subscribe to the four journals. A questionnaire was used to obtain the data needed for the study.

The evidence presented in this study indicates that reprography has no significant effect on the issue and is not the main reason for the loss of subscriptions of scientific journals in general and medical journals in particular.

For example, although the total sample could be considered representative of the population of subscribers to *Medicine*, only 22 percent of the respondents actually subscribe to it. One has to consider, of course, the general nature of this journal; nevertheless, it is evident that the great majority of potential subscribers do not subscribe to *Medicine*. The same holds true for *Pharmacological Reviews* (12 percent), *Journal of Immunology* (16 percent), and *Gastroenterology* (35 percent).

It is also evident that the majority of the pharmacologists (66 percent) do not subscribe to *Pharmacological Reviews* and over half of the immunologists (53 percent) do not subscribe to the *Journal of Immunology*. Also, 1 percent of the gastroenterologists are not subscribers to *Gastroenterology*. Being in a field of speciality, therefore, does not necessarily mean that the specialist subscribes to the journals relating to his field. On the other hand, evidence confirms the fact that cost and time are prohibiting factors in subscribing to scientific journals in general and to the above-mentioned four journals in particular. For example, the total number of respondents in the sample who do not subscribe to any of the four journals are shown in Table 7-1. Furthermore, it is evident that the availability of any of the four journals to nonsubscribers is the predominant reasons for their decision not to subscribe. The percentage varies for each journal and for the type of medium of availability, with libraries accounting for the highest percentage (59 percent for *Medicine*). Photocopying is a medium of availability of journals. The highest percentage of photocopy availability, however, among nonsubscribers was 11 percent (*Journal of Immunology*) followed by the availability through colleagues (4 percent for the *Journal of Immunology*).

TABLE 7-1

Total Number of Nonsubscribers To
Four Selected Journals

Journal	Never Subscribed	Dropped/ reduced	Total nonsubscribers
Medicine	229 (86%) +	36 (14%) =	265
Pharmacological Reviews	297 (99%) +	3 (1%) =	300
Journal of Immunology	278 (97%) +	9 (3%) =	288
Gastroenterology	215 (96%) +	8 (4%) =	223

Thus, one can discern that library service, in-house or through interlibrary loans, has a more positive effect on nonsubscribers to medical journals than does photocopying (see Tables 7-2 through 7-5).

Availability of the journal as a factor also holds true among those who dropped or reduced the number of their subscriptions. Other factors contribute to the situation in varying degrees. While photocopying was mentioned only in relation to *Medicine* as a reason for dropping three subscriptions, "too much to read" and "budget cuts" held the highest percentage, respectively, among previous subscribers ·to the four journals.

Although library service has a negative effect on subscriptions, librarians have played a positive role in introducing some subscribers to the four journals. It is also interesting to note that some of the subscribers to *Gastroenterology* and the *Journal of Immunology* were introduced to the two journals through photocopying.

Only two percent of the medical libraries dropped their subscriptions to two out of the four journals because of budget cuts. This indicates that photocopying and interlibrary loans have at most a negligible effect on the libraries' decision to subscribe to any of the four journals.

Almost one-third of all the respondents contributed articles to one of the four journals. However, in some cases, offprints of their works were provided to them at a price. On the other hand, 27 percent of the contributing respondents indicated that offprints of their contributions were no longer available.

In a very few instances the author owned the copyright on the work. Almost invariably the publisher secured the copyright to the published work. Some of the respondents in the sample did not even know who holds the copyright to their works. Exposure, therefore, can be considered the main objective of the author in the scientific world, whose concern is primarily to communicate his findings to his colleagues regardless of who owns the copyright on the publication.

TABLE 7-2

Total Number and Reasons For Not Subscribing to *Medicine*

	Total	Availability of the journal			Reason for not subscribing			
		Colleague	Library	Photocopies	Budget	Too much to read	Photocopies	Policy Change
Never subscribed	229	5 (2%)	135 (59%)	22 (10%)				
Dropped subscription	30	3 (10%)	23 (77%)		8 (27%)	24 (80%)	3 (10%)	2 (7%)
Reduced subscription	6	1 (17%)	5 (83%)		2 (33%)	5 (83%)		1 (17%)
Total	265							

These conclusions can be summarized as follows:

1. Lacking precise data from publishers regarding their profit maximizing, average costs, and marginal costs, one can conclude that photocopying, despite the claim of publishers of scientific journals, has little to do with the loss of subscriptions.

2. Library service and the availability of scientific journals in libraries have a positive impact on the user's decision not to subscribe to scientific journals.

3. Not all professionals and scholars subscribe to all the journals in their respective fields. The proliferation of scientific literature makes it impossible for any one individual to subscribe to all journals in his field. The rising cost of subscriptions and the time needed for reading are decisive factors in the user's decision not to subscribe to every given journal. Today's user is more critical and selective than his predecessor.

4. The scientist's main concern is to publish his findings regardless of who owns the copyright on them. The dissemination of his work, by any means, is more important to him than owning the copyright on it.

5. The need for information is the basis for the current practice among users of scientific journals. The declining cost of photocopies has no apparent influence on the user's copying practice.

6. Offprints of medical literature are not available for at least 27 percent of the published material.

7. Photocopying and the current interlibrary loan practice do not prevent medical libraries from subscribing to almost all medical journals.

TABLE 7-3

Total Number and Reasons for Not Subscribing
to *Pharmacological Reviews*

	Total	Availability of the journal			Reason for not subscribing			
		Colleague	Library	Photocopies	Budget	Too much to read	Photocopies	Policy change
Never subscribed	297	3 (1%)	124 (42%)	26 (9%)				
Dropped subscription	2	1 (50%)	2 (100%)	1 (50%)	1 (50%)	1 (50%)		
Reduced subscription	1					1 (100%)		
Total	300							

B. Possibilities for Further Investigation

The question of copyright is complex. Who is protected by the law? Is it the publisher or the author? Is it the society and/or the author? Or is it the society, the author, and the publisher?

There are many ways of approaching this issue and none is exact. This study was based on descriptive rather than experimental research, simply because the issue deals with events that happened in the past and will be affected by events that will occur in the future. Ideally, anything that deals with publications in general should be watched for a long period of time before an experimental study is undertaken. The investigator conducted the study at this time, however, with the hope that others will pursue the different parts of the issue in further investigations.

The question investigated here by no means covers the whole issue. Further valid questions should encompass the entire problem, assuming that the investigator has all the time and the data to devote to them. It is apparent that a single direction for all of the research would be too narrow. The writer chose a manageable part of the problem at this time to see if the research was on the right track and if at some future date further questions might be developed and investigated.

The Williams & Wilkins case is less significant than it might appear because there is no means at hand by which the publisher can control copying, which is now ubiquitous, except after the fact, when he has direct and legal evidence of the copying. Copyright, in this context, is the clue to a much larger issue which has not been contemplated. Is there any valid reason, in view of the development of copying devices and the lack of controls, for establishing photocopying as the norm of publication and producing copies only as needed through central agencies in given fields and by

TABLE 7-4

Total Number And Reasons For Not Subscribing
To *Journal of Immunology*

	Total	Availability of the journal				Reason for not subscribing		
		Colleague	Library	Photocopies	Budget	Too much to read	Photocopies	Policy change
Never subscribed	279	10 (4%)	122 (44%)	31 (11%)				
Dropped subscription	7	1 (14%)	3 (43%)		3 (43%)			
Reduced subscription	2				2 (100%)	5 (71%)		
Total	288							

means of automated networks? Granting that there is no change in the present state of development, commercial publishers of scientific and technical journals will find it extremely difficult to continue printing their publications in a periodical form. If such publication continues, it will probably be after an article has been read by those interested. Then the publisher will reprint a selected group of the most popular articles in a given subject area because the reprinted articles have given rise to other research and have been widely quoted.

Copyright serves as a clue to the future of commercial publication in periodical form. As it stands, the demand for scientific and technical journals will be highly specific and will continue as long as there are authors producing papers and readers eager to read them. The readership for any given article, however, will be much smaller than the subscription list of any periodical.

In this study, the writer was limited by the inability of the publishers to supply precise data and was compelled to investigate a part of the whole issue of scientific and technical publishing. The writer is well aware that this is much less than a complete statement. The part that was investigated simply shows that as far as we know, from the standpoint of the user, the availability of photocopying is not a reason for the user's decision to drop or reduce the number of his subscriptions; rather, his decision is due mainly to his limited time, constraint of budget, and narrowed interests. The user's report of his decision in the absence of other data can be accepted as truthful and the previous statement, therefore, appears to be valid. Thus, the initial supposition in this study is not supported, but it is clear from the evidence available that photocopying seems not to be the principal reason for the publisher's predicament of reduced subscription lists.

Despite the pending copyright bill, the writer is of the opinion that the whole concept of copyright will have

TABLE 7-5

Total Number And Reasons For Not Subscribing
To *Gastroenterology*

	Total	Availability of the journal			Reason for not subscribing			
		Colleague	Library	Photocopies	Budget	Too much to read	Photocopies	Policy change
Never subscribed	297	3 (1%)	124 (42%)	26 (9%)				
Dropped subscription	2	1 (50%)	2(100%)	1 (50%)	1 (50%)	1 (50%)		
Reduced subscription	1					1 (100%)		
Total	300							

to undergo considerable restructuring in order to produce a copyright law that meets the actuality of researchers who produce and use technical articles. In view of the devices that can substitute for publishing, the law may once again preserve the original purpose of copyright, which is the protection and reward of the author, whatever becomes of commercial publication, particularly of scientific and technical material.

The Williams & Wilkins court case and the difficulties of copyright represent a phase of the crisis rather than its substance. In watching what will occur in the next decade or more, the following elements should be investigated:

1. Journals in various areas of science and technology other than medicine should be investigated with regard to cost and readership.

2. The "twigging phenomenon," which refers to continuing specialization in publications, should be investigated and should be correlated with subscriptions and readership.

3. Further investigation should be conducted into the reasons given by readers for dropping or reducing the number of their subscriptions because the reliability of the data collected from the respondents in this study should be further tested.

4. A study should be undertaken of the copyright regulation in Scandinavian countries whose "Public Lending Rights" are implemented by law. The provisions, made to supplement the author's income on the basis of the use of his work in libraries open to the public, are in many ways similar to the suggestions of ways in which to

reach a possible settlement of the present controversy. There is an apparent conflict between the library's right to circulate materials and the author's right to be financially rewarded for his effort.

5. A portion of the studies devoted to the concept of networks and resource sharing should take into account the general problem of copyright and the principle of "Fair Use."

These and other possible areas of research require observation over a long period of time. Thus far, one can conclude that commercial publication of scientific and technical material and the concept of copyright are undergoing swift and radical change. The outcome remains in doubt, but the devices that occasioned the court case still exist and are becoming even more ubiquitous, and will be a concern of society far into the future.

NOTE

1. Nicholas L. Henry, "Copyright: Its Adequacy in Technological Societies." *Science* 186: 993 (Dec. 13, 1974).

Chapter 8

FUTURE COPYRIGHT LEGISLATION

The Supreme Court decision in the Williams & Wilkins court case does not signal, by any means, the end of the copyright controversy. Publishers and libraries have simply bought time until the next bout in court. The suggested workable clearance and licensing procedure in the meantime is not the only acceptable answer to all concerned. The crisis is here to stay as long as the original purpose of copyright is ignored. The question is whether anything can be done about the matter. The writer is of the opinion that the law which created the copyright could contribute to producing a solution by fully recognizing the historical reasons behind copyright, the intentions of the parties involved, and the public interest.

There is no doubt that the copyright concept and the law are undergoing some changes. Whatever the outcome of the pending copyright revision bill, however, the law should preserve the original purpose of copyright, which is the protection and acknowledgment of the creator's work regardless of what may become of the publisher. The main interest of many authors is to protect the integrity of their works. Profiting from the use of the work is secondary in many cases. The commercial publisher's interest, on the other hand, is to profit from the work.

One cannot deny the fact that the revision bill compensates for the lack of provisions in the current law in dealing with the new technologies and use. But the issue of enlarging the author's rights to cover every possible situation only means that the law will give more to the assignee.

The assignment of copyright is a unique concept in common law. Assuming that the purpose of copyright law in both common law and civil law countries is basically the same, it is interesting to note the divergent paths that have been chosen to achieve the desired end. The civil law looks primarily to the *creator* and the common law places its major emphasis on the *owner*.

Article 35 of the French law on literary and artistic property provides, for example, that an author must get a proportionate share of the receipts from the exploitation or sale of the work and that no lump sum payment is permitted. On the other hand, the pecuniary interests of the author under the present American copyright law are not prescribed by the statute, as are none of the other rights of assignment beyond simply permitting it. The U.S. Constitution empowers Congress to legislate in the field of copyright law. Nowhere in this charge does the Constitution indicate that promoting "the Progress of Science and useful Arts" should be achieved through financial remuneration or by considering copyrighted work as property best controlled through general property and contract principles. Nevertheless, this has become the basis of the American copyright law.

Civil law countries, however, base their copyright on the moral right of the creator (Droit Moral), a concept virtually unknown in Anglo-American law. In essence, it is the right of the creator, beyond his financial interest, to maintain some degree of control over his work regardless of the *ownership* of it. In the French law this right cannot be transferred, regardless of the contract language involved.(1) The most startling implication of the moral right, from the common law viewpoint, is the author's right to repudiate an assignment of his work.(2) He may, for example, withdraw his assignment even after publication, providing he is willing to compensate the assignee for losses.(3) The common application of this right comes in situations where an author feels that the publication of an early work may damage his reputation and acts to prevent it.

Anglo-American jurisprudence has not developed in a manner conducive to coexistence with a concept like "moral right." Property lies at the base of much of our law. It can be found in everything from marriage vows (to have and to hold) to homey maxims (possession is nine-tenths of the law).(4) Perhaps the esteem in which private property is held under the common law is best expressed by Blackstone:(5)

> The third absolute right, inherent in every Englishman is that of property.... The laws of England are therefore, in point of honour and justice, extremely watchful in ascertaining and protecting this right.... So great moreover is the regard of the law for private property, that it will not authorize the least violation of it; no, not even for the general good of the whole community.

While the last phrase in this statement may no longer hold true, it is true that entire areas of tort law have grown up to protect people from an owner's right to use his property as he pleases (for example, nuisance).

It is not surprising, therefore, that literary and artistic works are treated much as any other form of property in the common law. Once the property has been transferred, the creator ceases to have any control over it, in the absence of a contract to the contrary. This seems perfectly reasonable in the common law context.

The problem this attitude creates is obvious. While it is true that many authors write for financial remuneration only, most consider their works much more than a mere commodity to be bought and sold. In some fields, such as science and technology, the primary purpose of publication is frequently the dissemination of research findings. Yet much of journal publication is done without written contract between author and publisher, leaving the author at a decided disadvantage when he has turned over his work to be copyrighted by the publisher, because it is the owner of the copyright who decides when, how, and under what terms the work will be disseminated and when dissemination is no longer profitable. The inevitable question of disparity of power between the two parties is also apparent even with the existence of a contract. With the exception of the prominent writers who are sought after, publishers are generally in the position to dictate the terms of the contract, and the author has little choice in the situation if he wishes to disseminate his work. Although the American case law says that there is a difference between literary property and other types of property and that the author has rights on his work even if someone else holds a copyright on it, it is obvious that this is not the case because, in actual application of the law, general contract and property principles are applied and the contract reigns. Furthermore, the use of the words "copyright owner" throughout the text of the copyright law obscures the issue. The law should have provisions protecting the author per se.

Copyright is not a constitutional right. It is a statuatory right created by Congress and therefore may be changed or abolished altogether if Congress deems it necessary. It is a right created by law and enacted for the public good with the purpose of promoting science and useful arts. However, realistically speaking, the crux of the matter lies in designing provisions which "both encourage the creation of original works and permit, in the meantime, the widest possible access to dissemination of information to the public."(6) When these goals compete the legislator should strike a balance which best serves the main objective of promoting learning, scholarship, and the arts; after all, copyright was not intended to be used as a vehicle for commercial ventures. Furthermore, the law exacts no correlative legal duties to balance the copyright owner's monopoly over his work. In fact, the interest of the public is taken care of as an incident to the copyright owner. The fundamental objective of copyright is the public good and the legislator's duty is to preserve this priority.

The interests of the three parties (author, publisher, and public), nevertheless, are interdependent and must be identified if we are to develop an effective and acceptable copyright law. Dealing with all three parties under one law confuses the issue and adds to the problem.

Another area of consideration is "fair use," a nebulous concept which is unclear even to the jurists. This judically created concept compensates for the lack of recognition, on the part of the existing law, of the fact that the reproduction of portions of a copyrighted work for the purpose of scholarship and research is desirable. The concept has been in use by libraries for many years but it lacks the assurance of freedom of liability from unjustified law suits. Recognizing the doctrine and practice, the legislators incorporated "fair use" into Section 107 of the revision bill. The language of the bill, nevertheless, is general and the court has to decide in every case whether the user's copying is an infringement or fair use. Fair use, therefore, as it stands, is not really the right to copy under certain criteria, but a defense to be evoked if one is sued. The language of the revision bill may invite harassing and unjustifiable suits, and it does not contribute to peace and understanding between the parties involved in the copyright issue. Fair use should be stated as a right and not as a defense mechanism.

On the other hand, it is interesting to note that Section 108(g) of the revision bill states that the rights of reproduction do not extend to a library which "engages in the systematic reproduction" of copyrighted materials. Although the term "systematic reproduction" has not been defined, one tends to believe that it may refer to reproduction practiced by information networks. It is rather confusing to permit a library to reproduce copyrighted material for a research purpose and on the other hand to prohibit such reproduction for the same purpose if the said library becomes a member of a network. The revision bill should consider the reasons behind library cooperation. The question involves both the right of access to information by the public and the cost of that access.

As previously mentioned, the author must write for the publisher to publish and the public must buy if the publisher is to publish. Granting that financial rewards have to be acknowledged and recognized (lest we lose touch with reality), it is clear from the author's viewpoint that the availability and dissemination of his work comes before financial rewards in order or priority. The ownership of copyright, therefore, must be identified. Equally important is the recognition of the nature of the copyrighted work and, accordingly, the extent of protection. There is no reason why two sets of protection-time cannot be introduced, the shorter of which should pertain to the publisher. In addition, the legislator should seriously consider the nonavailability of a copyrighted work as grounds for a forfeiture of the copyright. After all, the work belongs to society and ultimately ends up in its domain.

The present legislation if it becomes law, even with the changes recommended here, will not answer all the questions that may arise in the future. The greatest

mistake is to consider copyright a closed issue as soon
as a law is passed. As knowledge itself is dynamic,
so must its protection be. Beyond the pending legislation, we need to establish a new basis for copyright
that takes greater account of the public's right to knowledge and the author's desire that his work be disseminated. So far, copyright law has favored the commercial publisher and his need for profit to the point of
forgetting that the publisher is the servant of the
authors and their public, deserving a reward for his
efforts but not to be made the master of the process
by which knowledge is produced and utilized.

NOTES

1. F. G. Guttman, "Droit Moral of the Author Under French
   and German Law." *Journal of Business Law*
   p. 157 (1969)

2. French law on literary and artistic property, article 29.

3. *Ibid.*, article 32.

4. Marycatherine Reed, "Assignments of copyright," unpublished
   course paper, LS 279. Graduate School of Library
   and Information Sciences, University of Pittsburgh,
   Spring, 1975.

5. *Blackstone's Commentaries on the Law of England.* Oxford:
   Clarenden Press, MDCCLXV 1765, Vol. 1.

6. Edmond Low, "What Edmond Low Told the House Sub-
   Committee About Libraries." *American Libraries*
   6: 410-411 (July-August 1975).

BIBLIOGRAPHY

Allen, S.; Green, S.; Friedman, J.; Harrington, B.; Johnson, L. "New Technology and the Law of Copyright: Reprography and Computers." *UCLA Law Review* 15: 938-1030 (April 15, 1968).

American Library Association. *Interlibrary Cooperation.* Chicago: American Library Association, 1967.

Becker, Joseph, ed. *Proceedings of the Conference on Interlibrary Communications and Information Networks, Airlie House, Sept. 28-Oct. 2, 1970.* Chicago: American Library Association, 1971.

Benjamin, Curtis G. "Soaring Prices and Sinking Sales of Scientific Monography." *Science* 183: 238 (Jan. 25, 1974).

Berg, Sanford V. "Structure, Behavior and Performance in the Scientific Journal Market," Ph.D. dissertation. New Haven, Conn.: Yale Univ. 1970.

Blasingame, Ralph, "The Great Library in Sky Prototype." *Library Journal* 97: 1771 (May 15, 1972).

Bowker, Robert R. *Copyright: Its History and Its Law.* New York: Houghton Mifflin Co., 1912.

Breyer, S. "The Uneasy Case for Copyright: A Study of Copyright in Books, Photocopies and Computer Programs." *Harvard Law Review* 84: 281-351 (Dec. 1970).

Brinkley, R. D., *Manual on Methods of Reproducing Research Materials.* Ann Arbor, Mich.: Edwards Brothers Inc., 1936.

Brooks, John. "Profiles, xerox xerox xerox xerox." *New Yorker* 63: 46-90 (April 1, 1967).

Brown, N. B. "Price Indexes for 1974." *Library Journal* 99: 1775-1779 (July 1974).

Bush, George P., ed. *Technology and Copyright.* Mt. Airy, Md.: Lomond Systems Inc., 1972.

Cambridge Research Institute. *Omnibus Copyright Revision: Cooperative Analysis of the Issues.* Washington, D. C.: American Society for Information Science, 1973.

Campbell, T. H., and Edmisten, J. *Characteristics of Scientific Journals–1962.* Washington, D. C.: Herner & Co., 1965.

Chapin, R. E. "Limits of Local Self-Sufficiency." In *Proceedings of the Conference on Interlibrary Communications and Information Networks,* edited by Joseph Becker, p. 54. Chicago: American Library Association, 1971.

Clapp, V. W. *The Future of the Research Library.* Urbana, Ill.: University of Illinois Press, 1964.

—————*Copyright–A Librarian's View.* Washington, D. C.: Association of Research Libraries, 1968.

Committee on Scientific & Technical Communication (SATCOM). *Report of the Task Group on the Economics of Primary Publication.* Washington, D. C.: National Academy of Science, 1970.

Committee on Scientific and Technical Communication of the National Academy of Engineering. *Scientific and Technical Communication: A Pressing National Problem and Recommendations for Its Solution.* Washington, D. C.: National Academy of Science, 1969.

Desola Price, D. J. *Science Since Babylon.* New Haven: Yale Univ. Press, 1961.

Dessauer, John H. *My Years With Xerox.* New York: Doubleday, 1971.

"Fair Use in Photocopying: Report on Single Copies." *ALA Bulletin* 55: 572 (June 1961).

Federal Funds for Research, Development, and Other Scientific Activities, Fiscal Year 1971, 1972 and 1973. Washington, D. C.: National Science Foundation, 1972.

Fetterman, John J. "Resource Sharing in Libraries–Why?" In *Resource Sharing in Libraries,* edited by Allen Kent. New York: Marcel Dekker, 1974.

Goldman, Abe A. "The Concept of the Law of Copyright." In *Reprography and Copyright Law,* edited by L. Hattery and G. Bush. Rochelle Park, N. J.: Hayden Book Co., 1973.

Gosnell, Charles F. "The Copying Grab Bag: Observation on the New Copyright Legislation." *ALA Bulletin* 60: 46-47 (Jan. 1966).

————"Copyright." In *Copying Methods Manual,* Edited by W. R. Hawken, pp. 309-316. Chicago: American Library Association, 1966.

Hattery, Lowell H., and Bush, George P. *Technological Change in Printing and Publishing.* Rochelle Park, N. J.: Hayden Book Co., 1973.

Henry, Nicholas L. "Copyright, Public Policy and Information Technology." *Science* 183: 384-391 (Feb. 1, 1974)

————"Copyright: Its Adequacy in Technological Societies." *Science* 186: 993-1004 (Dec. 13, 1974).

Huang, Te-Hsien. *Bibliography on Copyright.* Halifax, Nova Scotia: The Compiler, 1972.

Hurt, Robert M., and Schuchman, Robert. "The Economic Rationale of Copyright." *American Economic Review* 61: 421-432 (May, 1966).

Ibrahim, Karen. "Exploring the Meaning of 'Reprography.' " *Graphic Arts Progress* 16: 10-12 (1969).

Keenan, Stella, and Stillman, Mary E., eds. "The Copyright Controversy: Issues and Opinions." *Drexel Library Quarterly* 8: 377-602 (Oct. 1972).

Knight, Douglas M., and Nourse, E. Shepley, eds. *Libraries at Large.* New York: Bowker, 1969.

Koepke, J. C. "Assessment of Documentation Practices in Reprography." In *Reprography and Copyright Law,* edited by L. Hattery and G. Bush, pp. 50-58. Washington, D. C.: American Institute of Biological Sciences, 1964.

Kuney, Joseph H. "Economics of Journal Publishing." *American Documentation* 14: 238-240 (July 1963).

Lacy, D. "The Economics of Publishing." *Daedalus.* 92: 42-62 (Winter 1963).

Latman, Alan A. "Fair Use of Copyrighted Works." Study 14, March 1958, Committee on the Judiciary, U.S. Senate, 1960. U.S. Congress, 86th, 2nd Session, "Copyright Law Revision." Study 14, prepared for the Subcommittee on Patent, Trade-works and Copyrights, Committee on the Judiciary, U.S. Senate. Washington, D. C.: U.S. Government Printing Office, 1960.

Libraries and Copyright: A Summary of the Arguments for Library Photocopying. Chicago: American Library Association, June 1974.

Lukac, George H., ed. *Copyright: The Librarian and the Law.* New Brunswick, N. J.: Rutgers University Graduate School of Library Service, Bureau of Library and Information Science Research, 1972.

Macaulay, Thomas Babington. *Macaulay's Speeches on Copyright and Lincoln's Address at Cooper Union, Together with Abridgment of Parliamentary Debates of 1841 and 1842 on Copyright, and Extracts from Douglas's Columbus Speech.* edited by Charles Robert Gaston. New York: Ginn and Co., 1941.

Marke, Julius J. "Copyright Revisited." *Wilson Library Bulletin* 42: 35-44 (Sep. 1967).

————*Copyright and Intellectual Property.* New York: Fund for the Advancement of Education, 1967.

Matthews, Glenn E. "Photocopying." *Encyclopedia Americana.* Vol. 22, pp. 1-11g. New York: Americana Corp., 1973.

Mooers, Calvin N. "Computer Software and Copyright." *Computing Surveys* 7: 45-72 (March 1975).

Moon, Eric. "Satisfaction Point." *Library Journal* 93: 1947 (May 15, 1968).

Mount, Douglas N. "Copyright: The Situation Now." *Publishers Weekly* 199: 24-27 (July 5, 1971).

Overhage, Carl. "Plans for Project Intrex." *Science* 152: 1021-1037 (May 20, 1966).

Paige, L. J. *A Special Report on the Means of Financing Mathematical Journals.* Providence, R. I.: American Mathematical Society, 1963.

Passano, William M. "How Photocopying Pollutes Sci-Tech Publishing." *Publishers Weekly* 197: 63-64 (Feb. 2, 1970).

Pforzheimer, W. L. "Historical Prospective on Copyright Law and Fair Use." In *Reprography and Copyright Law,* edited by L. Hattery and G. Bush, pp. 18-35. Washington, D. C.: American Institute of Biological Sciences, 1964.

Price, Miles O. "Photocopying by Libraries and Copyright: A Precis." *Library Trends* 8: 432-447 (Jan. 1960).

Report of the Register of Copyrights on the General Revision of the U. S. Copyright Law House Committee on the Judiciary. 87th Congress, 1st Session, 5 (Committee Print, 1961).

"Round Two: Supreme Court Appeal." *American Libraries* 5: 60 (Feb. 1974).

Saunders, J. S. "Origin of the Gentleman's Agreement of 1935." In *Reprography and Copyright Law,* edited by L. Hattery and G. Bush, pp. 159-174. Washington, D. C.: American Institute of Biological Sciences, 1964.

Shaw, Ralph. *Literary Property in the United States.* Metuchen, N. J.: Scarecrow Press, 1950.

————"Publication and Distribution of Scientific Literature." *College and Research Library* 17: 293-303 (July 1956)

————"Williams & Wilkins v. the United States." *American Libraries* 3: 987-999 (Oct. 1972).

Shipman, Joseph C. "Collection Building." In *Encyclopedia of Library and Information Science,* edited by Allen Kent and Harold Lancour, Vol. 5, p. 260. New York: Marcel Dekker, 1971.

Sophar, Gerald J., and Heilprin, Lawrance B. *The Determination of Legal Facts and Economic Guideposts with Respect to the Dissemination of Scientific and Educational Information as It is Affected by Copyright–A Status Report.* Prepared under Project 7-0793, Contract OEC-1-7-070793-3559 for Bureau of Research, Office of Education, Department of Health, Education and Welfare, Dec. 1967.

Stephanie, Mary. "A History of the Interlibrary Loan Code." *Wisconsin Library Bulletin* 57: 272-275 (Sep.-Oct. 1961).

Survey of Copyrighted Material Reproduction Practices in Scientific and Technical Fields. Chicago: George Fry & Associates, 1962.

Tallman, Johanna Elenore. "Opinion Paper: An Affirmative Statement on Copyright Debate." *Journal of the American Society for Information Science* 25: 145-150 (May-June 1974).

U.S. Copyright Office. *Copyright Law Revision Studies Prepared for the Subcommittee on Patents, Trademarks and Copyrights of the Committee on the Judiciary United States Senate.* Study 15, 86th Congress, 2nd Session (Committee Print, 1960).

The Williams & Wilkins Company v. *The United States.* The United States Government of Claims, Report of Commissioner James F. Davis to the Court, No. 73-68, Feb. 16, 1972.

INDEX

A

A. B. Dick Company, 5
Advertising, 16, 18, 108, 110, 111
Advertising revenue, 121
Allergists, 133, 135
American Association of Gastroentrologists, 125, 132
American Association of Immunologists, 125, 132
American Association of Junior Colleges, 35
American Association of Law Libraries, 35, 77, 94
American Association of Law Schools, 35
American Board of Allergy, 133
American Board of Internal Medicine, 133
American Council of Learned Societies, 32
American Institute of Physics, 109
American Library Association, 9, 33, 34, 35, 36, 38, 66, 77, 94
American Library Association, Reference Services Division, 39

American Library Association membership, 110
American Society of Pharmacological and Experimental Therapeutics, 133
AngloAmerican Law, 154
Assignability, 52
Assignee, 154, 155
Assignment, 87, 154, 155
Association of American Publishers, Inc., 77
Association of Research Libraries, 33, 35, 94
Author, 52, 84, 85, 99, 109, 137, 142, 146, 148, 150, 157
Author right, 151
Authors League of America, Inc., 77
Audit Bureau of Circulation, 19
Availability, 134, 141, 144, 148
Availability, non, 158

B

Back issues, 17, 111
Biomedical literature, 43
Biomedicine, 111
Blanket copyright, 84